Knots of Eternity
Paradoxes from Dadi to Daughter

Volume 1

Dadi Darshan Dharma

Printed and bound in Canada by Transcontinental, March 2007

© *Knots of Eternity. Paradoxes from Dadi to Daughter.* Volume I

ISBN: 978-0-9734439-3-6

© 2007 Orange Palm Publications
Registration of copyright: first trimester 2007
National Library of Quebec
National Library of Canada

Mailing address: Orange Palm Publications©
235 Rene Levesque Boulevard, Suite 310, Montreal, Quebec, H2X 1N8
Telephone: (514) 255-8700 ~ Facsimile: (514) 255-0478
E-mail: info@palmpublications.com;
Website: http://www.palmpublications.com

Graphic design and illustrations: D.D.D., Lucie Robitaille, Eric Mathieu, and Jocelyne Beaudry
Typesetting: Louise Roy
Book cover: Photo by Simhananda
Jacket cover: Photo by Gaétan A. Brouillard

All rights reserved. No part of this book may be reproduced in any form without permission in writing from the author except to quote, or photocopy specific passages for the purposes of group study.

Publications by Orange Palm Publications:

Buddhas, Bodhisattvas, Khadromas and the Way of the Pilgrim — A Transformative Book of Photography and Pithy Sayings (in three languages). Simhananda. 2007.

Holy-Moly Hiccoughs and Enigmatic Knotty Eructations From the Boffola Belly of Bu'Tai. The Drôleries and Dictums of Crazy Modern Dzog-zen. Ken N.O. Sho. 2007.

The Smiling Forehead — Paradoxes from Dadi to Daughter. Volume 2. Dadi Darshan Dharma. 2007.

The Great Golden Garland of Gampopa's Sublime Considerations on the Supreme Path — Contemplative Contemporary Commentaries of Gampopa's Root Text. Volume 1. B. Simhananda 2005.

Paradisal Plums: Peaceful Ponderings from a (Rebel) Pandit's Puce Palm — Aphorisms, Adages, and Analects of Sri Adi Dadi, Volumes 1, 2. Etbonan Karta. 2001.

Forthcoming books:

Flyers from the Boys in the Buddhafield. B. Simhananda.

Paradisal Plums: Peaceful Ponderings from a (Rebel) Pandit's Puce Palm, — Aphorisms, Adages, and Analects of Sri Adi Dadi, Volumes 3, 4. Etbonan Karta.

Publications by Magnificent Magus Publications:

The Divine Concordance of Light III: The Science of Full Moon Invocations from Humanity's *Heart to* Hierarchy's *Will*. Etbonan Karta. 2007.

Seven Studies of Soul Stations or Soul-ar Progressions Upon Each of the Seven Cosmic-Physical Rays (an integral excerpt from Collectanea One, *The Divine Concordance of Light*). Etbonan Karta. 2007.

Seven Sacred Stations of the Self & Seven Flaming Fiats of Light Upon the Seven Cosmic-Physical Rays (an integral excerpt from *The Divine Concordance of Light*). Etbonan Karta. 2001.

The Divine Concordance of Light: A Handbook from Heaven to Progression Earth — "The Seven Rays of God: Seven Studies of the Soul's Earthly Pilgrimage of Service Upon the Seven Cosmic-Physical Rays". Etbonan Karta. 2001.

Forthcoming books:

Scriptings of the Soul in Questions of Light. Dadi Darshan Dharma.

The Divine Concordance of Light II: The Science of Invocation and the Art of Affirmation from Station Humanity *to* Hierarchy's *Heart*. Etbonan Karta.

Dedication

"To the Enlightened Fool in all of us."

Special Thanks:

Firstly, thank you to Lou for working so closely and devotedly with the author on this special project; thanks also to the dynamic duo of Light-Bulb Luce and Jyoti Joss for the attentive aid given in the great graphic designs and setting of the book's inspired layout; and what can one say about Luce and Jyoti's insightful drawings and inspired illustrations except, "Wow!" Next on the list to be rightly recognized and sincerely thanked is our own Divine Mamma Jo-zee, for her constant encouragement and support of everyone, and for playing the roles of both the eagle-eyed supervisor and mother-hen vis-à-vis the project. And finally, we have Eric the enlightened idea man to thank for the colorful cover design, and our Doc Gaetan for kindly providing for everyone's enjoyment, the inspired front-cover photograph. Thank you to all, visible and invisible, who have helped, or have had an impact upon this book in its various stages of production.

With Blessings and affection,

D.D.D.

Table of Contents

Foreword ix
I.   Treasure Box 1
II.   Mystery Box 13
III. A Care-Enough Parcel Box .25
IV. Leaves Upon the Grass 37
V.   Humble-Humus of Buddha-Mind 49
VI. Strange Seeings 61
VII. Spiritual Postcards 75
VIII. The Power of Grace and The Clap of Compassion 89
IX. Seeds of Light and Shade 101
X.   Bubble Gum & Betty Boopers 125
XI. Blinkins' 137
XII. Divine Ascriptions 149
XIII. Inspired Imputations 161
XIV. Rusty Hinges 173
Glossary 185

Foreword

The Occidental Master, Dadi Darshan Dharma is a living, laughing buddha of authentic spirituality, and a veritable paradox of the magical verb.

Although a being of great simplicity, his writings reveal to the world a complex wisdom and a spirit of the greatest refinement.

All of the paradoxes and precepts which pepper and enliven this unique book with their light, humor, and surprising depth, act as master keys which can suddenly open doors to many unsuspected aspects of the Truth within-us-all.

Dadi Darshan's pen impels us to question even the most mundane issues in our lives. His thoughts constantly short-circuit our deeply entrenched thought patterns and belief systems. He metaphorically sets the living pages about the Spiritual Path on fire with a desire for the Divine, now.

Dadi dares us to 'be Faultless in fault', to be 'Patient in our impatience', to 'laugh with the tears of the thunderstorm', to be 'jealously un-jealous', to be 'Securely insecure' and to be 'a Saint right down deep into sin'. He mentions off-handedly that "Because you yearned for the Answer, He Handed you the Question", and astutely, he comments that "Because you opened your Eye, He saw Himself".

These paradoxes and precepts are both a wonder and a wake-up call. They mysteriously realign with vigor, seriousness, and fun, our mind's modulations with that of the Spirit's High Vision, (or Dharma View), and they give us a new world-perspective vis-à-vis some immortal truths and common spiritual concepts.

Dadi magically manages to touch our inner Heart in a loving fashion and he Lightly gives the 'Happy Smile' back, once again, to its original owner, the Soul.

May you enjoy this heavenly treasure drove of cosmic chocolate delicacies which are the Paradoxes and Precepts of Dadi as much as I did, and may you 'take time to read it and reflect upon it, even if you don't have time'.

It will not be wasted nor will you regret it.

Yours in Light and Wisdom,

Josée D. Senécal
Chief Editor
Paume de Saint-Germain Publishing Inc.

"When the glad gaze of God grazes your smiling forehead, you gracefully give unto Him your grateful ghost."

D.D.D.

Treasure Box

I

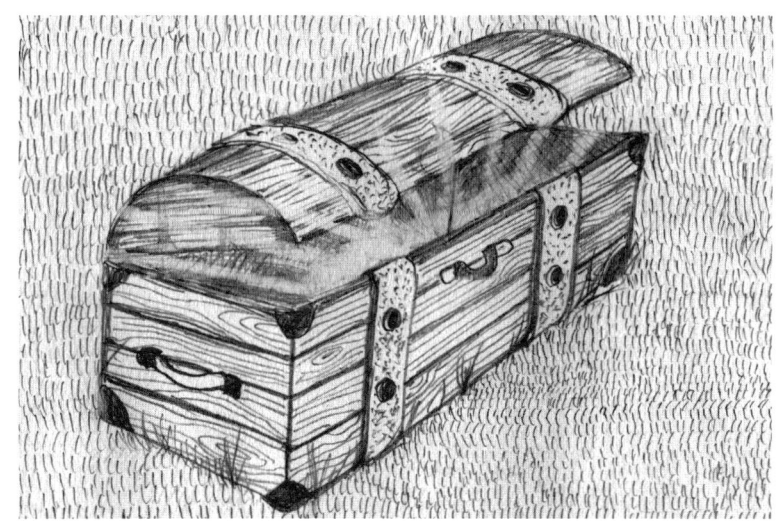

Knots of Eternity
Paradoxes from Dadi to Daughter

Treasure Box

Learn to be Patient with your impatience.

Learn to shoulder your lack of peace, Peacefully.

Learn to remain Calm in your anger.

Learn to be Content in your lack of happiness.

Treasure Box

Learn to be utterly Compassionate in your humble lack of understanding.

Learn to be pointedly Compassionate toward all sentient beings vis-à-vis your acknowledged deficiency of discerning discrimination in the gray zones and subtle areas of world affairs, internal politics, and interplanetary possibilities.

Learn to be profoundly Compassionate in your obvious lack of visionary perspective vis-à-vis Hierarchical Purpose, especially in respect to the planned evolution of Light and Clarity within the human Mind.

Learn to be more Understanding in your secretly avowed urban intolerance.

Learn to be charitably skillful in the handling of any kind of ingenuously subtle bias.

Learn to be lovingly kind and compassionately comprehensive, in all cultivated predilection shown toward anything whatsoever.

Learn to be openly Affectionate though you may still lack love.

Learn to be Gentle in spite of the spontaneous awaring of anger; and to be Meek in spite of the sudden arising of aggressiveness.

Learn to be Loving even as jealousy rears up its horny hooves, once again.

Learn to be Satisfied though most always unappeased.

Learn to be restful in Divinity, or relaxed in the Nature of Mind, without ever having attained to God, or Emptiness.

Learn to be detached from attachment, and more importantly, not attached to detachment.

Learn to be serious, humorously; and grave, lightfully.

Learn to fear heroically; and to tremble calmly.

Learn to be Kind to your imperfections and to become impeccably Imperfect.

Learn to carry the Angel within you down to the pits of manifest Hell.

Learn to be devilishly Good even when it's time to be bad.

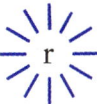

Learn to forgive and forgive again as people keep killing you again and again.

Learn to aim for the bulls-eye of Truth, even through your habitual propensity to lie.

Learn to pray for all those wealthy who have stayed poor.

Learn to contemplate consciously and meditate one-pointedly, even as someone stomps hard on your little toe.

Learn to Rejoice in equipoise and to cry Calmly even as someone heartlessly smites your subtle sensitivity and harshly hurts your susceptible feelings.

Learn to be Attentive to your lack of attention and to be mindful of your lack of Mindfulness.

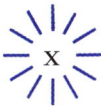

Learn to Ignore your ignorance and consecrate yourself to your Omniscience.

Learn to be a Saint right down deep into sin.

Learn to be your Self even when you are not.

Mystery Box

II

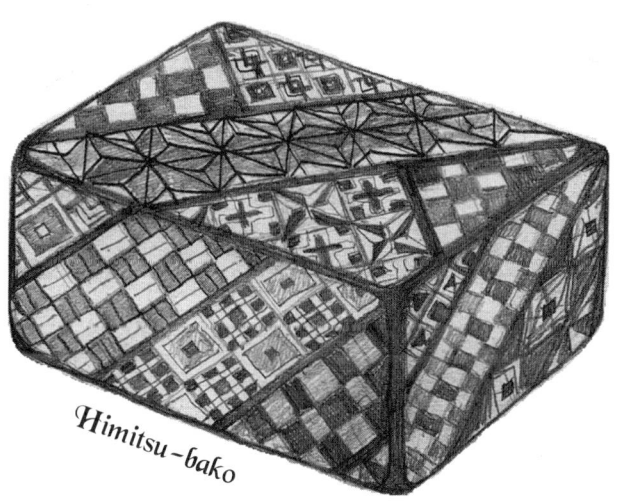
Himitsu-bako

Knots of Eternity
Paradoxes from Dadi to Daughter

Mystery Box

Dare to let the Divine Fool dictate worldly wisdom to you.

Dare to be Spiritually bored, and like it.

Dare to love despite all contrary conditions.

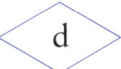

Dare to be Buddha-like in spite of all ego-sumptions.

Mystery Box

Dare to be dove-like even as you take a tough stand.

Dare to laugh with the tears of the thunderstorm.

Dare to Smile through the throes of a heart-twister.

Dare to go on when only quitting calls.

Dare to do discipline whenever *tamas* is in tantrum.

Dare to Sadhana when spirituality sucks.

Dare to Contemplation, whenever, wherever, and however impossible.

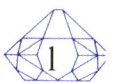

Dare to Pray earnestly even when sitting on a pin-point.

Dare to be jealously un-jealous.

Dare to be Securely insecure.

Dare to be Joyfully sad, (if need be).

Dare to be depressingly glad for another's good fortune, again.

Dare to be Successful, failure after failure.

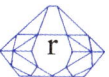

Dare to take the next step even if your feet are bound in cement.

Dare to be Intelligent in spite of your stupidity.

Dare to be adroitly dumb in true Wisdom.

Dare to be Faultless in fault; and full of fault even though Faultless.

Dare to be spent, not preserved; dare to be consumed, not conserved.

Dare to be a *no body* instead of a body; dare for your spirit to Care, even if *nobody* does.

Dare to Chant (Mantra) whenever the inner dialogue goes on and on non-stop, or whenever the song of Self goes disenchantingly off-key.

Dare to die while Life is bloomingly alive and full of trumpet and sound.

Dare to Live when all which is inside wishes only to die.

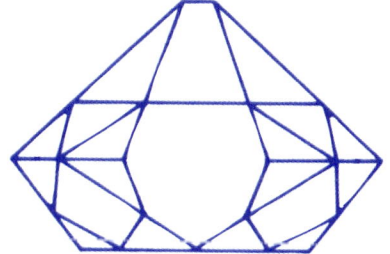

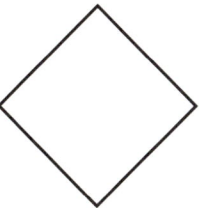

A CARE-Enough Parcel Box

III

Knots of Eternity

Paradoxes from Dadi to Daughter

A CARE-Enough Parcel Box

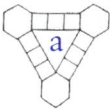

Care enough to take time even when you don't have time.

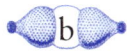

Care enough to be a real Builder even at the obvious risk of being bonged by an obtusely blind somebody's brick.

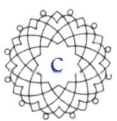

Care enough to keep on doing guileless Good even when morally criticized of alleged opportunism, or smugly accused of something equally risible, like rampant egoism.

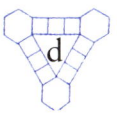

Care enough to stay steadfast when in personal crisis, and of course, fully devoted when assailed by Doubt.

A CARE-Enough Parcel Box

Care enough to be fully Dynamic when fatigue assaults, and intrinsically Healthy when sickness plagues.

Care enough to give more and more of efficient Energy, especially so, when it appears that the dynamic spirit of your personal daemon, has been spirited away.

Care enough to let go of your assumptions, opinions, persuasions, principles, creeds and beliefs, especially so, if you seriously care to climb over the stiff cliff of self-conceit.

Care enough to give an attentive no-ear to the din and clamor of Silence... especially so, to the unbroken call of Emptiness.

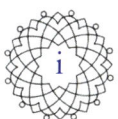

Care enough to selflessly serve and render ardent aid today, whenever and wherever needed, even if tomorrow could very well be callously cruel and leave you high and dry, terribly torn and worn down, unjustly injured, and quite forlornly forgotten.

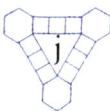

Care enough to be sincere, honest and true even as somebody's lie corrosively betrays your pure intention and smears your sterling disposition.

Care enough to be patient in Excellence even as middling minds and spineless spirits sorely surround, bridle, and bore you... (hopefully), to perdition.

Care enough to be simple and to keep it Simple, even if you are intelligently complex, esoterically wise, and spiritually complete.

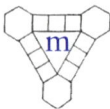

Care enough to make sure that you always Love more than you can possibly be hated.

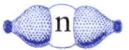

Care enough to fully inhale Life as it flashes by, and care enough to exhale It as being planetary precious upon your outbreath.

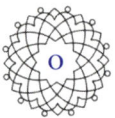

Care enough to get to know God right where you are, before He can possibly escape into the next moment.

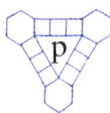

Care enough to Believe even in those who blindly believe.

Care enough to feed the hungry of Spirit, even as they strike your hand hard with their considerable cynicism, and spiritual materialism.

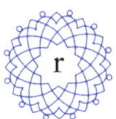

Care enough to absorb all willful contention upon the Path, as being simply a natural reaction belonging to the pure pleasure of free Opposition.

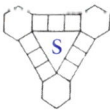

Care enough for your Being to bless the world and to bless your neighbor's blond boy even as he undissimulatingly steps, and cloddishly clip-clops all over your beautifully, newly-sown lawn, to get his damnably bewitching red ball out of the plain, pregnant dirt.

Care enough to wondrous world works, peppered with a generous kindling of kindness and a plentiful sharing of Goodwill, even as the human mob rolls over you and bops you but good.

Care enough to communicate compassionately with an open Clarity, even when the state of your Heart is a palpably open wound.

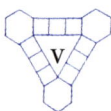

Care enough to do your Divine Best, even if that Best gets you exactly zilch in attention, and even less in Recognition.

Care enough to shed the skin of your past, even as the immediate Present slinks a new casing along the serpentine unknown of your Future.

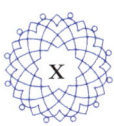

Care enough to want to metamorphose your life, even as you ponder upon the imponderable wonder and sweet odor and humble beauty of an everyday jasmine flower, held ever so lightly in the crucible of your hand.

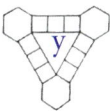

Care enough to say Thank You even if the situation absolutely stinks.

Care enough to care because you have taken care to Care, and for no other apparent reason.

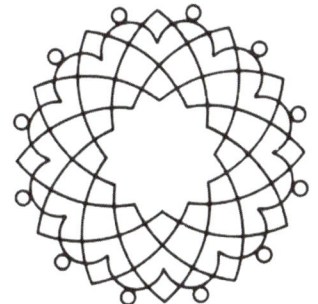

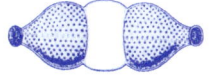

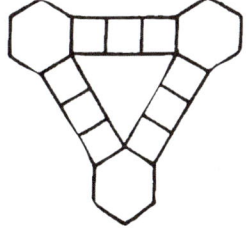

Leaves Upon the Grass

IV

Knots of Eternity

Paradoxes from Dadi to Daughter

Leaves Upon the Grass

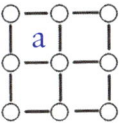

Do not forget, (nor neglect), someone, nor something that should have been done, in your sometimes misplaced hurry, to reach the Sacred Goal.

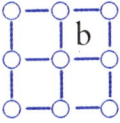

Do no forget, (nor neglect), the fact that only your hollowness can make place for His Hallowness.

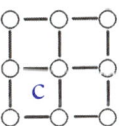

Do not forget, (nor neglect), to look as deeply as possible into His Will, every time, before receiving Instruction.

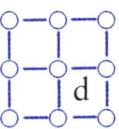

Do not forget, (nor neglect), that all of life is the Last Supper.

Leaves upon the Grass

Do not forget, (nor neglect), that the reading of scriptures can never replace the Mindful Eating of a good bowl of rice.

Do not forget, (nor neglect), the spiritual need to accompany the Christ to your Cross, and then, to die there yourself.

Do not forget, (nor neglect), that you must learn the disciplinary task of *walking uncrossed upon your crossed self,* in order to be able to reel-in the "Razor's Edge" from out of the existing chaos of your ordered life.

Do not forget, (nor neglect), that you must drink directly from His Cup, in order to savor the One Taste of His Wine.

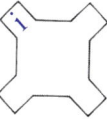

Do not forget, (nor neglect), that you only get to live Life starting the day you have ceased to sleepwalk to the toilet, and most notably, from the very moment you (have) decided to desist, from somnambulating away the rest of your super-exciting *subexistence*.

Do not forget, (nor neglect), the necessity of letting go of all claims, if the Real is ever to be Reclaimed.

Do not forget, (nor neglect), to abstract your name again and again, upon the pure emptiness of each Charlie Brown Sigh.

Do not forget, (nor neglect), that you must deftly defy the defiance of the mind, whilst the Soul passionately challenges the complacency of the self.

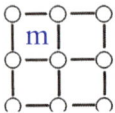

Do not forget, (nor neglect), to note that the Sex Solution is antiseptically asexual.

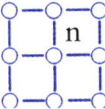

Do not forget, (nor neglect), to commit yourself unconditionally to the gentle, discerning Agape which summarily sends all attacks and criticisms scurrying shamefaced and subdued… into Silence.

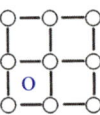

Do not forget, (nor neglect), to take into account that Inclusiveness excludes exclusiveness, yet ever includes it.

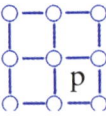

Do not forget, (nor neglect), that it is the Seeker's relentless, but relaxed Quest, which spontaneously spawns the Holy Spirit.

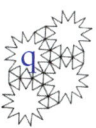

Do not forget, (nor neglect), to detect that Nir-vana spills out sempiternally spontaneous into Samsara and into the spiritual life of the sadhaka, as impeccable Samaya and perfect Sat-sangha.

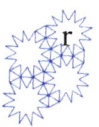

Do not forget, (nor neglect), to behold that the Buddha boldly embodied your humble body at birth.

Do not forget, (nor neglect), the truth that the Christ meditatively selected your noble Heart to transmit His Love, through the unassuming Empty Casing you have naturally inherited, and Spiritually cultivated.

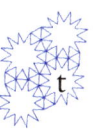

Do not forget, (nor neglect), that you must practice the Practice daily, assiduously, and without tiring... yet do the all of it, *effortlessly*.

Do not forget, (nor neglect), that the Lord needs you as much as a hole needs space, in order to Be.

Do not forget, (nor neglect), that true Awareness can radically annihilate murder by allowing the garden of the mind to grow only the tender sprouts of Ahimsa.

Do not forget, (nor neglect), that you must consciously crystallize the basic self into one solid block of Unalloyed Lead, before the Great Undertaking of alchemically transforming it, into a majestic, pyramidal SELF of Pure Gold.

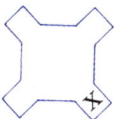

Do not forget, (nor neglect), to cognize your 'Sangha Community' as embodying a 'Collective Merit' re-activated, and displaying a 'Group-Grace', recouped.

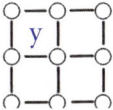

Do not forget, (nor neglect), to recognize that the Long Island Line to PERFECTION is travelled upon intermediate cargo rails of Imperfection.

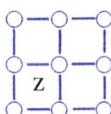

Do not forget, (nor neglect), the occult fact and magical formula that it is Kindness which allows the Path to appear, and you to disappear.

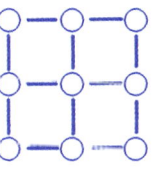

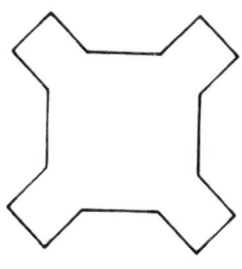

Humble-Humus of Buddha-Mind

V

Knots of Eternity

Paradoxes from Dadi to Daughter

Humble-Humus of BUDDHA-Mind

Note that to bind yourself to a belief is to betray the Buddha.

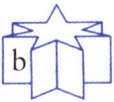

Note that the Lord finds Life only as He Awakens in your Heart.

Note that the Master's words are never more true than when he goes into their opposite mode, or moves into their antithetical mood.

Note that your enemy serves you well.

Humble-Humus of Buddha-Mind

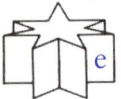

Note that a quiet despair demarcates the dungeon into which a disciple fell into temptation with his ego's full acclamation.

Note that doubt is dauntless. Doubt waits in a dark crouch to snatch the Soul's cry, caught anguishing in every disciple's throat at the time of test and trial.

Note that for each thought of hurt and every act of wound wrought out in the world, the selfless sadhaka seeks to counteract each with a kindling Compassion filling his every thought, and a comely Kindness conditioning his every move.

Note that the first precept of the disciple is to let LIFE Be.

Note that the second precept of the disciple is to let LOVE through.

Note that the third precept of the disciple is to let LIGHT abound.

Note that the fourth precept of the disciple is to let LIFE, LOVE and LIGHT brightly blend and move as ONE-Flame within his Heart of HEARTS.

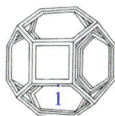

Note that the peaceful promontory of a detached, attentive Presence is the supreme nectar to be dispensed to all those who are in critical need of Love's cultivation.

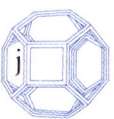

Note that in order to transmit Love to another, you must *Be* there right now... before you two ever meet.

Note that all Real communication begins with the goodness in your heart being dispatched to another upon the Zen-bow of your (pure) Intention.

Note that the polite prop of proper Listening should positively precede the power of proper Speech.

Note that a mother enfolds her crying baby in arms of Motherly Love; so also, ought the disciple enfold each of his faults, when these cry out to him in dire pain (of attention).

Note that the disciple who claims to dialogue with God never gets to know His *Real Essence*, nor His *True Name*.

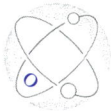

Note that the perfidious protagonist, Death, is but a pretender to power over LIFE.

The true disciple who dies never gets to feel Death's sudden chill, or calling card.

He just drops calmly down to the ground, and lays himself to rest like a leaf, into the humble humus of Nature's BUDDHA-Mind.

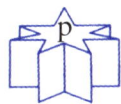

Note that if you deeply touch your Original Face, it will reveal to you but the Mask of God.

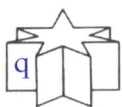

Note that if you deeply look into the Great Yoni, you will see Seminal CREATION in gestation.

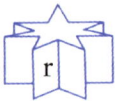

Note that if you dip deeply into your disciple-body, you will find your own Soul smiling back at you from every pore.

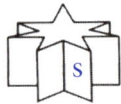

Note that the so-called faults and seeming weaknesses of a genuine Buddha are His most perfect tools of disciple teaching, training and transmission.

Note that the Purity of an authentic Master knows no moral code of conduct.

The behavioral modality of such a Being comports itself consistently with supreme Spontaneity, correct Impeccability, just Cause, and superior Reason.

Note that to the right of all directions is to be found the Bright Buddha of Bodhicitta, (Avalokiteshwara); and to the left of all directions are to be found the twined Compassionate Princesses of Bodhicitta, the 'White Tara' and the 'Green Tara'... who are ever caring, ever helping and ever bestowing blessings, protection, and mercy upon this originally pure, but presently needy and wanting planet.

All bone fide disciples should prostrate themselves to this piously Divine Triplicity, deeply, promptly and unpretentiously.

All people should humbly petition Their pardon, prayers and protection; and concomitantly, desire a genuinely Deep Peace for all sentient beings to sagely profit by.

All who are presently ready and wise enough should Awaken now, and expeditiously esteem and celebrate Them.

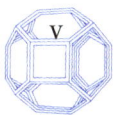

Note that the time you think you have is not really the time that you Really have, in order to do what you have to Do, before it all runs out, along with you.

Note that Peace soup can only be made by you becoming a humble pea.

Note that Superior Spirituality is simply Supreme Love.

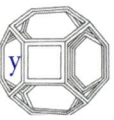

Note that for the accomplished disciple who constantly remembers LOVE, God is all there Is To Do.

Note that the discipline of Spiritual Sadhana is all the search you shall ever need, in order to extract the process of the Dharma PATH from out of the sacrificial throes of the fast-becoming empty shell of an already *dying self*.

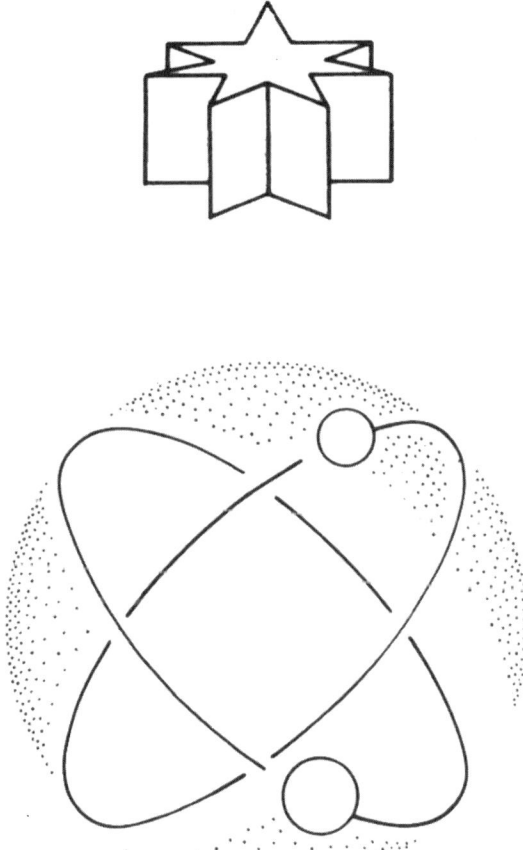

Strange Seeings

VI

Knots of Eternity

Paradoxes from Dadi to Daughter

Strange Seeings

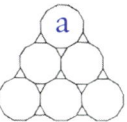

So strange to see how the soft soul seems to swing significantly to where the smiles are.

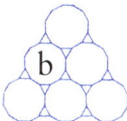

So strange to see how the impotent soul is inclined to recline upon a dime of pseudo-passion and take pleasure (in the luxury) of lascivious laxity.

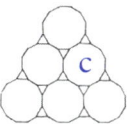

So strange to see how the insubstantial soul dresses up the small self with an ofttimes obsessional skin of superficial security and shallow happiness.

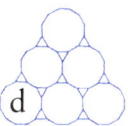

So strange to see how the half-hearted, half-heard and shy soul, so often strives to summon out of life only the self-subsisting pianissimos of gentle gest and tender-talk.

Strange Seeings

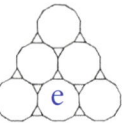

So strange to see how resentment can harden a once loving heart; and bitterness empoison a once affable nature; and rancor destroy a once open mind.

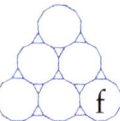

So strange to see how one who suffers much usually learns much; but how much more suffering there is, to see the pain of one who never learns.

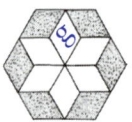

So strange to see how through the multiple ministerings of a Masterfully-managed *meltdown* of the ordinary 'I-mind', and by the simultaneous *softening* process of a disciple's multivariegated experiences of 'trial-by-Fire', there is to be potently disclosed the pure, double-edged 'Mind-Sword' of Soul-ar discernment and Self-detachment.

So strange to see how the stinging strikes and savage slashes of intentionally wounding Speech, can so cruelly tear to agonizing shreds the tender human Heart; and so ruthlessly, violate the fundamental respect for our Being and the very divinity of our Soul... deeper by far, than any jagged wound discharged from the slicing sword of any physical abuse.

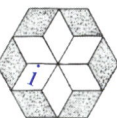

So strange to see how two holy humming, hidden hands create the Clap of God, but how only one has to disappear, to Hear the Hand of SHAMBALLA's Will tapping reverently and purposefully, upon the *Sushumna nadi*, or central channel, of the spine.

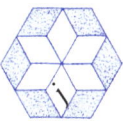

So strange to see how short a life can be, but how mysteriously long, a sweet smile can last.

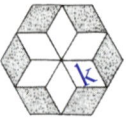

So strange to see how Hate blinks-on the bad and how Love blinks-on the good; but how much more rare is the Unblinking Eye that can justly behold both beams, and in so doing, bequeath an unbiased Compassion.

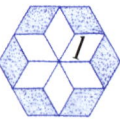

So strange to see how the DIVINE MOTHER Loves with an Equal Vision that which is Divinely-superior, as well as that which is Divinely-ordinary; and, furthermore, the Divinely-wealthy, as well as the Divinely-poor; and the Divinely-creative, as well as the Divinely-destructive; and the Divinely-friendly, as well as the Divinely-hostile.

All-Inclusive and All Is Well... in the Divine Mother's Vision of LOVE.

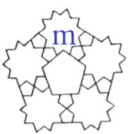

So strange to see how the Feminine Mystique can only be demystified Mystically and led to Liberation, Occultly.

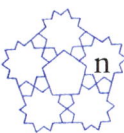

So strange to see how a truckload of unrestricted desires is able to leave the passionate recipient, still palpitatingly Unsatisfied, yet so satiated.

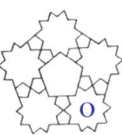

So strange to see how the serpent of seeming kindness and the snake of warm words can mysteriously woo, and even bring one who has the character of a carcajou, to woe.

So strange to see how a clanging moment of impatience can crash the next speeding second (of existence) to a catastrophic stop; and how a mere mindful moment of superior patience, can bring the second hand of possible adversity to a standstill.

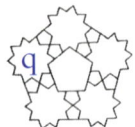

So strange to see how one creative cloudburst of Pure Joy pouring out GOD upon our Being, can disperse in one Seized Second, the accumulated musty air of a thousand years of sorrow.

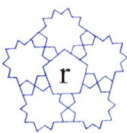

So strange to see how the Gander of God cannot be gotten without the stratagem of stalking the Breath with the gamble of Death.

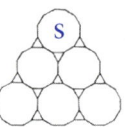

So strange to see how a life of modest Simplicity can shyly shape, and highly hoist, the holy host of Happiness.

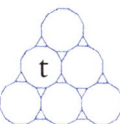

So strange to see how no sooner said than wrapped-up, is the wondrous work of a *woman of worth*.

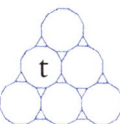

So strange to see how the serviceable lover who supremely Loves, adjudges no service too adverse, nor sacrifice too severe, to be sustained for the sake of the Beloved.

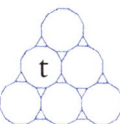

So strange to see how the simplest resistance to Divine Work increases sevenfold the pain, effort, and time it takes to bring about Its Resolution.

So strange to see how the simplest resistance to even one tiny Divine task has about the same, proportionately-relative, repercussion.

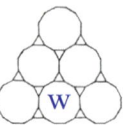

So strange to see how seriously a disciple goes about demanding Sri Doodadi's blessing for this and for that desired doodad, but how in fact, the occidental sadhaka does so preciously little to sincerely, (and seriously), deserve it.

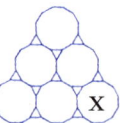

So strange to see how the bark of a Master, so often turns into a bouquet of roses, upon the altar of a keenly receptive heart.

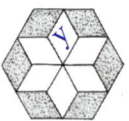

So strange to see how he who criticizes his brother, or censures his sister, gets quietly segregated from the Sangha of the BUDDHA.

<u>The Spiritual Fool</u>:

So strange to see how the more pompous and delusionary a spiritual fool is, the more stupidly intelligent, (or intelligently stupid), and the more stupendously Sightless, is that man (or woman), inclined to become Spiritually.

The spiritual fool tends to fill his consciousness to the cusp with a subterfuged 'self-will', which he surreptitiously graffitis everywhere along the cracked corridors of his openly-contracted existence.

The spiritual fool covertly cavorts with his ingenious self alone, in a one-way logorrhea of thought, speech and act, but notwithstanding, he does so, in a pretended show of Presence, (dialogue and communication), with other.

So strange to see such a patently spiritual saphead, acting pseudo-adroitly in a slick, psychic and egoic personality style which is both brazenly bold and uppishly bald; and how, with a sincere, albeit unconscious, self-persona and a pallet of nasty, narcissistic brushstrokes of bland romantic rose and dull eminent brown, the aforesaid spiritual fool is able to *paint-express* himself forth as someone of utterly exquisite sensitiveness; and to top it all off, as a phony luminary, he can bewitchingly concoct or mysteriously trump up, the image of an almost perfect persona of superior, (albeit selfish), selflessness.

The spiritual fool tends to envision himself as incarnating into material view, an obviously noble sacrificial life, the likes of which, is *humbly* messianic in breadth.

In resume, the spiritual fool, will more or less, outpicture himself to be an esoteric student of supreme perceptibility and superior purpose, and he will naturally (try to) transpire forth an incomparable calmness and superb transpicuity.

In other words, he will magically incant and magnetically objectify the subjectively created self-image of being a godly and goodly brother upon the Dharma Path… who is somehow able to see everything with a high definition of crisp cosmic clarity, and with the merited superiority of the most grandiloquent B.S. of spiritual sorts.

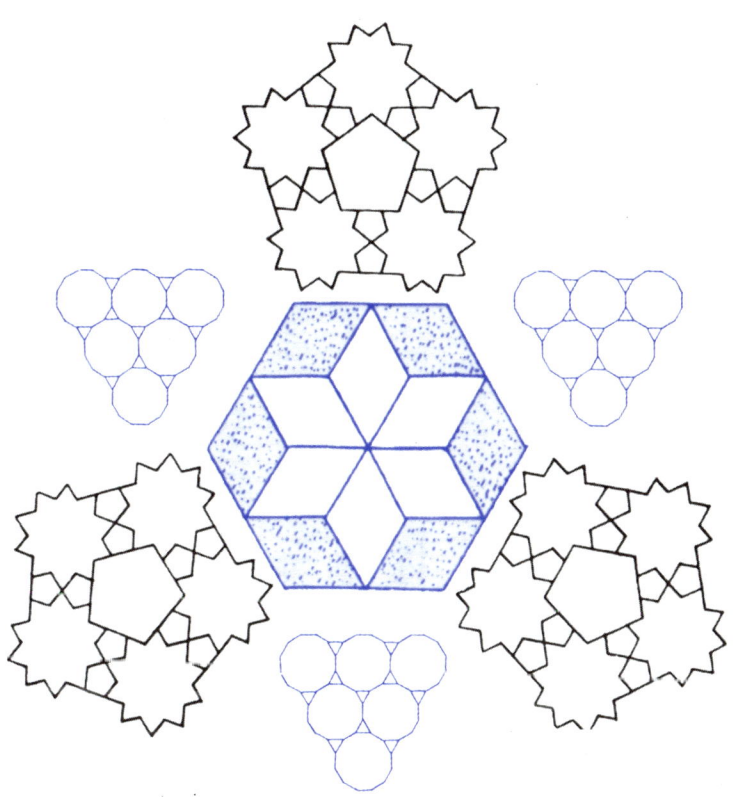

Spiritual Postcards

VII

Knots of Eternity

Paradoxes from Dadi to Daughter

Spiritual Postcards

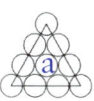

Who can say that within an insignificant mount of rock, or an unseeming pile of primordial stone, there hides not the ADI SHIVA Himself, in a cryptical crouch of unshackled Power and unbounded Bliss?

There is no width nor length, no height nor bottom, no horizon nor nadir, to the Task of Loving.

Pain is the prasad of Purusha skillfully extracting karma.

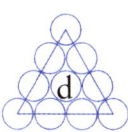

The world may be maya, but *this* is no mere sunset.

Spiritual Postcards

As the Holy Helmsman of the Heart, HARE HARI hauls *aham* hushly into the heavenly Harbor of HRIDAYAM.

Blissfully Naked was the DIVINE MOTHER until She mercifully donned the Dress of MAYA for the sake, the salvation, and the festivity of our Probationary Planet and its courageously Cloaked Souls.

The poisonous arrow that we string and send toward another, mysteriously and mercilessly pierces our own Heart.

Agitation for GOD makes us need Him all the more as we press on relentlessly in our heedless *heat* to Reach HIM.

It is from His Sacred HEART of the purest Cool Compassion, that He will choose to pose His Hand of Guarding Grace upon our fiery forehead, and still our SOUL's Divinely-fevered pace.

It is from His Boundless HEART of most Bountiful Baraka that the marvelous mystery of Unspeakable Peace is likely to *painfully* pierce our Heart and to implode LIGHT everywhere Ineffable and forever Lambent into the enormously *empty* space(s) of our BEING.

Enigmatically, we are not wont to need anything Evermore… except perhaps, the strange Necessity to lay an Eternally present, purified Tear at His Glorified Feet.

Hard times hail the best from a holy Heart; Peaceful times hail precisely the undaunted same.

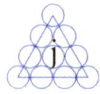

Sleeping side by side lie the Opposite Poles and though seeming enemies of force by day, they share the same bed of Ennobling Equilibrium, by night.

In relating perfectly to God in all human relationships, whether they be presently harmonious or difficult, the all of it proceeds in perfect commensuration with the unwinding karma of a relatively interdependent, human-connectedness… uprightly happening and correctly composing itself within a spiritually polarized, finally expiring cycle of experiential samsara, for both self and other.

From out of a Light-impregnated sadhana coming to natural term in the calmness of a transparent Clarity, are inaugurated the labor pains of the color-pregnant *rainbow arc* and *rainbow body*, which lionheartedly presage the ineluctable Birth of a BUDDHA.

To lose yourself in GOD is to locate your self in Life.

MOTHER MARY is the Divine Dispenser of the sacred currency of GRACE coming out of CHRIST's Universal Bank of Compassion.

The Body of GOD lies just beyond the 'Objective Obvious' of self-corporeality (in man).

The Spirit of GOD lies just beyond the 'Subjective Sense' of the intuitive perception of Self (in man).

The Intent of GOD lies just beyond the 'Obligatory Oblation' of the Soul's SELF, as being 'Naturally Naught' (in man).

When the glad gaze of God grazes your smiling forehead, you gracefully give unto Him your grateful ghost.

If only you knew all of another's pain, pride would nevermore hurt another Heart.

All sadhana, discipline, training, instruction and teaching, unfolds as a sealed, Sacred Scroll of progressively Divine Revelation, etherically scribbled unto the Total Mind of all incarnated Consciousness, by the Earthfire Intent of none other than, 'the LIFE of HIM in Whom we live, move and have our being'.

Love brightens the eye, enlightens the thought, lightens the understanding, enlivens the existence, and quickens the life.

May the Dove of Love alight with Its Light all abright into the night of your life.

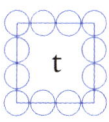

On this particularly good day which is today, the stalwart pilgrim uplifts the world high with his awe-inspiring, spiritual strength.

But on the very next (awful) day, the gross world presses down despairingly upon him with its onerous samsaric substantiality.

SPIRITUALITY is not the pumping of Psychic-iron.

All That Is God, is naturally beyond all Duality-barbells.

If baneful speech burns etherically upon your tongue, let there erupt from your throat, a Baptismal Bonfire of Silent Sound.

So let all past bitter words of resentment and recrimination be Radiantly Reborn into benign blossoms of Beauty and blameless bits of (Buddha) Bright.

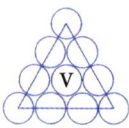

Clearly, religion is the politics of those whose essence is naturally devotional and who wish to be ritually Saved.

Plainly, politics is the religion of those whose subjective nature is passionately visionary and who utopically, want to be Free.

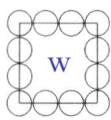

The first lesson to be mastered in the mystical art of innerly 'Listening to God' is that of decelerating the inner dialogue and curbing the outer speech.

The second lesson to be mastered is, indeed, quite simple in essence but absolutely spartan in practice... it is that of skillfully instoring the occult, corrective cure of Silence.

The bright Inner Sun blazes darkly and even the Nameless Name forgets to Shine, when a son of Mind becomes dumb and blind to the chime and twinkle of Life's Laughter.

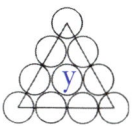

Tranquil insightful meditation smites with discernment and exactitude, the undisciplined ball of thought... that is to say, the subjectively-contracted, comparatively continual, 'I-centered', inner dialogue.

But then the solid, inner whack of right contact with (our) essence racket, or spirit bat, oddly brings on an Instant Silence, and swiftly escorts the meritorious man, towards the gift of what the Buddha impeccably coined, 'right action', or 'correct comportment'.

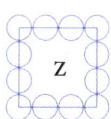

The Naked Truth of SPIRIT was essentially a radiant core of Pure Emptiness before Creation ever was, and the Soul even stirred.

SPIRIT will never cease to Be and I shall never cease to Love IT, without beginning and without end... till the present Dream that seems to be the *now* disappears forever into the *never was*... and the Essence of LIFE asserts Itself to be *Only-the-Effulgent-*ME, tumbling down to earth in playful titters of Absolute Glee.

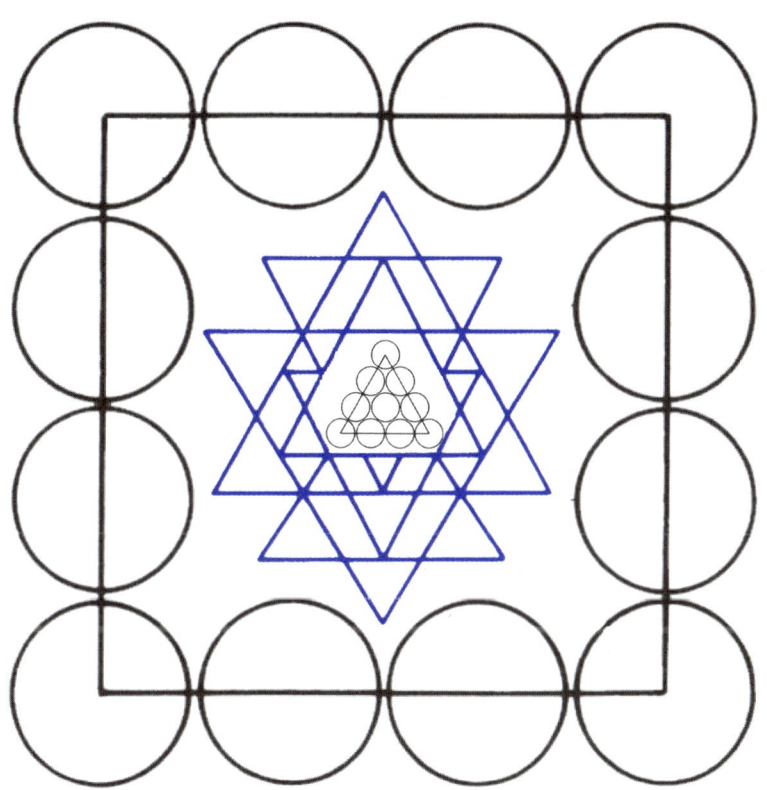

The Power of Grace and The Clap of Compassion

VIII

Knots of Eternity

Paradoxes from Dadi to Daughter

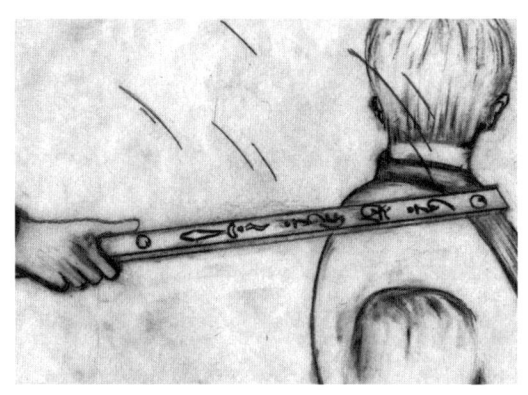

The Power of Grace and
The Clap of Compassion

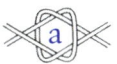

The mind must be mounted and Mastered as if it were of no-mind... which, of course, it is.

Hatred harasses, hostility haunts, hindrances hamstring and hardness harpoons heartlessly the hypocrite who half-heartedly, (or elsewise, under contentious circumstance), heinously hunts down the HOLY.

Compassion circumambulates around a bodhi-enlightened Mindful Meditator, somewhat like a disciple who deep-circles in tranquil equanimity around a Buddha.

May I meditate as magnificently immaculate as a pure grain of white rice, solitarily alone on a lonely white shelf of some quite insignificant, white-clapped cupboard which was long ago forsaken, and which now lies quite forgotten and exquisitely frozen, under the snow-cap of a barely accessible, ivory-white glacier.

The Ultimate Healing is the hauling down of the scaffolding of thought at Will and then falling down thoughtless and empty, into the warm chalice of Kwan Yin's unbounded compassion.

In much the same way that Count Dracula is unable to find his reflection, Colonel Ego has never been found able to substantiate his shadow.

The sobering shock of the subsisting flow and flux of form flowing fluidly into the frieze of samsara frightens a budding Buddha into being Already Free.

To the pig the impure apple of the world appears just as godly good to gobble as it would seem to the sanctimonious hypocrite, who out of covert covetousness parsimoniously eyes a polluted plum of the Spirit.

Uncleanliness uncloaks itself as being concupiscently *clean* to the ungodly cadet.

Uncleanness also uncloaks itself as being clearly *Clean* to the Immaculate Chaitanya.

The discarded rags of the self are bemusedly sewn into the saffron dress of the Saint.

The sinner sees the unreal as real and the Real as fiendishly false; the Saint sees the unreal as unreal and the Real as Really Real.

Albeit, both viewpoints must perforce be taken to test, and must necessarily toil upon the Toilet of Truth... prior to the GREAT FLUSHING.

Passion permutes the personality and pummels the Spirit of the puny person, the prime perpetrator being the profane apostasy of an Uncultivated mind.

Mind the mind so that *Maya* and *Mara* may maze and amaze no more.

God-talk without practice sadly short-circuits spirituality to no-shares in GOD-Stock.

Unfix the self from the flypaper of subjectivity and fly far and free as a subjective Butterfly of Objectivity.

The Unsleeping die not, but the sleepy do dodo, and duly die.

The ever-present pleasure of a Noble Mind is to delight in the conscious awaring of the passage of every passing mini-moment of Vigilance.

The dam of self-Mastery keeps all fatal floods of runaway feeling at bay.

Unmindfulness regales in heady heedlessness.

Mindfulness heeds and heels-in, only Wisdom.

To become intimate with Desire is to court attachment.

To court *attachment* is to risk getting caught and crunched by the crocodile maws of this yet unsacred world.

Though ever a kingly resident of Sacred Mount Meru which soars far above the vale of sorrow and tears, the bold Bodhisattva of Bodhicitta regularly treks down into the valley of human endeavor, (and ungodly suffering), for a Compassionately-shared tin can of good tomato soup, generously sprinkled with Buddha-alphabits.

Do not be so bedeviled by the Buddha as to forget your Budh-ingly, boring buddy.

A drunkard of Divinity drops deep into the hell of Heaven.

To forsake sin is to surrender desire and to discard virtue is to abandon fear.

The cohering gold dust of a self-conscious divinity, transposes into the shiny pestilence of a prideful sadhaka who, alas, has become Divinely-sick.

Plain pity without the *pow* of Grace and a little mercy without the *clap* of Compassion underscores the *service* of perhaps a hard-driving, but essentially non-forgotten self, or else, it punctuates the impotent *sacrifice* of a blindly devotional, yet still, un-Mastered self.

Seeds of Light and Shade

IX

Knots of Eternity

Paradoxes from Dadi to Daughter

Seeds of Light and Shade

Distorted desire does more to disadvantage the mind of a disciple than the diatribes of an adversary.

Impure intent impales the heart of a disciple far deeper than the iniquitous inflictions of an enemy.

Greater good than from your helpless self can your Divine Mind deliver to your hapless halfwit.

An ordinary man depends on things and others for his greater well-being and happiness.

The Awakened man recognizes that it is none but *Other-as-Self,* who is the intimate cause of his Real Being and Only Happiness.

Be Free, not spiritual; be Empty, not self; be Monadic, not divine.

All is vanity, for all vanishes. But all that vanishes ceases to be mere vanity, if consciously construed by a Soul whose quiet centre is *shunyata*.

The spontaneous arising of the thought life out of nothing must be creatively applied toward the constructive harmony and beatific beautification of the world, no matter what happens in Life... and this, always through the honorable wherewithal of a disinterested, Noble View.

Whom among you will collate my words of Wisdom, and place them as delicate, cultivated flowers in a Vase of Truth?

Whom among you after a predestined time, will dare to 'shatter the vase', and gather to himself the empowered seeds of (their) Light, for the greater good and salient benefit of all sentient beings.

In putting AHIMSA into practice, be like a beatifically busy bee.

Strike out from Heaven's Hive and buzz busily Bright and joyfully Aware from yellow flower to blue flower and from human field to Buddha field... and back again, to the great golden Hive of Heaven, all aglow and blissfully exultant.

The disciplined sadhaka must learn to inject into any outer Happening the practiced partaking of the precisely right amount of precious *spiritual pollen* taken from the core of his Floral Being, without ever harming the outer *prarabdha* petals of his prim and spiritually primed, personality Petunia.

Amidst the dust of mortal kind, OH, the sparkle of a disciple!

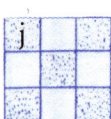

Sweet to the Spirit is incense and joss, but sweeter still to the *Buddha of Fragrance,* is the attar of Innocence.

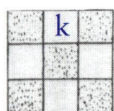

Bad manners, bad behavior, bad company and bad carrots in a black bag don't necessarily make the world Bad.

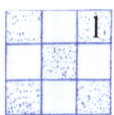

The unwise never seem to desire a keen and correct understanding of the why, when, where, and however, they are sometimes, (so very) 'wrong'... and who really cares?

These unwise ones, therefore, do not honestly 'do' anything much about it, since they deceptively pretend to ignore, or simply to be (somehow) unaware, of the *hefty responsibility* of 'being wrong'.

The wise, however, '<u>get it</u>' every time that they are... 'in the wrong'.

And these wise ones, very much 'on-the-spot' desire to repair and restore, and do something *constructive* about it every time... over and over again, however which way they must... until the all of it has been *responsibly* 'righted'.

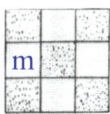

Illumination is not an inundation of darkness with Light, but demonstrates rather, a *cool, calming Clarity*.

Enlightenment is not a state full of flash and fulgor, but is first and foremost, a simple, cold, and clear *Effulgence of Awareness*.

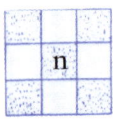

An enlightened fool's illumined folly fields the field of lofty philosophy as if it were the fictitious filibusterings of only half-luminary fools; furthermore, the enlightened fool, in his fiery Fabianistic folly, fingers all foray of unillumined feats and unaware functionings as being frail, frivolous, fatuitous, and foolish foofaraw.

The following favor of savory sagacity passes as a free forewarning, to-and-against, 'the keeping of copious company with a foreseeable fool'.

FRUGAL FOREWARNING:

"If you fool about rashly with a fatuous fool, you do feckless foolery, you get forlornly fooled, and you finally finish up, a fearless foolproof fool!"

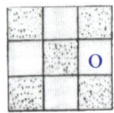

Dare to desire fame and glory twicely unmindful and you double the detour to the Dokhma.

Dare to desire dumb Adam in the darkness of your (ever-) young Yoni, again and again unconsciously, and you double-dutch the Dark Angel.

And, by the shades of Hades, and lost in the dank arms of Morpheus, you make place for a dour date with Yowling YAMA, the ravaging, rapacious Lord of Death.

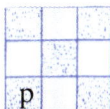

Spiritual pride sends the Soul scurrying deeply back into the grotto of *Savikalpa Samadhi*.

Occult ostentation sends the Self scuttling deeply back into the cavern of *Navikalpa Samadhi*.

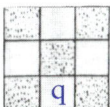

The plural games of the world spell out well the many names of Delusion.

The preponderancy of gambling in the world gyres deftly the delusory handle of Deception.

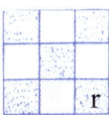

More and more goods, more and more wealth; more and more desire, more and more children.

Isn't the planet plenty Plump enough?

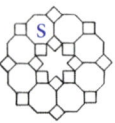

More procreation, more poverty, more pain, more despair.
Isn't the earth Embarrassed enough?

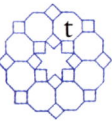

A disciple reaches Illumination to *shine* in the Dark.

An Initiate attains Enlightenment simply to dispel the Darkness.

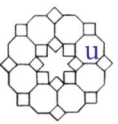

DIVINE DUNDERPATE THEOREMS

The unconscious fool is a fool in fact. He is 'asininely' alive.
The semi-conscious fool is oft befooled. He is 'avidly' alive.
The Conscious fool is a Cultivated Fool. He is 'always' alive.
The Supraconscious fool is a Superlative Fool. He is 'awesomely' alive.

CUTE FLORAL COROLLARIES

The total fool is a deadpan Dandelion's *bud in-the-buff*.

The partial fool is a dandified Daisy's *burgeon with bluff*.

The Aware Fool is an aroused Rose's *bouquet in bloom*.

The Radiant Fool is a dignified Delphinium's *acrospire in Alleluia*.

INCORRIGIBLY-CRUDE COROLLARIES
(For the Spiritually-Sturdy Only!)

The born fool is a *burro's* ass_ _ _ _!

The oxymoronic fool is an *ox's* ass_ _ _ _!

The Awakened Fool is *his own* ass_ _ _ _!

The Perfect Fool is Everybody's ass- - - -!

TRANSFINITE AND TRANSCENDENTAL COROLLARIES

The Transfigured Fool is a hallowed *Burning Bush* in the middle of Nowhere.

The Illumined Fool is a beatific *Firefly with Wings of* OM... foolishly-flapping Japa Mahanam as true JNANA-Marg.

The Enlightened Fool is a desert *Sagebrush caught Afire*, and Laughing (Madly) across the Sands of Time.

The radically-Aware, Effulgent Fool is an Extra-Luminescent *Lingam of Loveliness*... *lila*-lullabying the Goddess's *Yoni of Light* to Liberty... with the Lash of the LORD's Love for Life.

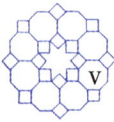

One must become absolutely capable of discerning, whether or not, the pointing finger which considers to personally criticize a present point of human incarnated Light, points (also) to that which is *beyond* the accosted speck of sparkle on the human horizon, to include imminently the Sea of Seminal SPLENDOR.

To be claimed by the Clarity of TRUTH is to proclaim a perfect Peace even in the midst of an encroaching personal darkness, lasting a thousand-and-one days of dreamless sleep.

But to be claimed by a toxiferous criticalness and to bandy about words of vengeance and to decry in angry laments, and to catapult evil thoughts in harm towards others, is to drag the bad, the damned and the ugly into bed with you, and to fall fathomlessly forsaken each night into a frightful and a fitful sleep, replete with wholesale darkness and unforgiving dreams.

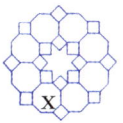

Before you, as a competent *sadhaka*, can confidently pull-up your Packard-*sadhana* by the roadside with enough Spiritual Power in tow to boost-charge a Brother/Sister motorist upon the Dharma Path, remember first, to fix-up your own modest, flat tire of 'Tired Divinity'.

You, as the experienced and skillful *sadhaka* on the Road of Return to GOD's Garage in the Inner Sky of the *Subjective Beyond*, can be of real Bodhisattva help only:

1. after you get out of the deceptive ditch of... DISTORTION, (DELUSION & DISILLUSION).

2. after you get out of the designing ditch of... DISTINCTION, (DELINEATION & DESTINY).

3. after you get out of the defeatist ditch of... DIFFIDENCE, (DISINCLINATION & DEFLECTION).

4. after you get out of the distrustful ditch of... DOUBT, (DUBIETY & DISBELIEF).

5. after you get out of the divagating ditch of... DIGRESSION, (DISCURSION & DIFFUSION).

6. after you get out of the diffractive ditch of... DISPERSION, (DEVIATION & DIVERGENCE).

7. after you get out of the displeasing ditch of... DISAGREEMENT, (DISCREPANCY & DISPARITY).

8. after you get out of the disparaging ditch of... DERISION, (DISRESPECT & DISREGARD).

9. after you get out of the disarraying ditch of... DESIRE, (DELIGHT & DISSATISFACTION).

10. after you get out of the disquieting ditch of... DISTRAUGHTNESS, (DISCONCERTION & DETONATION).

11. after you get out of the disjunctive ditch of... DISUNITY, (DISORGANIZATION & DISORDERLINESS).

12. after you get out of the deceitful ditch of... DISHONESTY, (DUPLICITY & DOUBLE-DEALING).

13. after you get out of the ditzy ditch of... DISTRACTEDNESS, (DISCOMBOBULATION & DAYDREAM).

14. after you get out of the dolorous ditch of... DETERIORATION, (DECLINE & DEBILITY).

15. after you get out of the dunghill ditch of... DECEPTION, (DISINGENUITY & DISLOYALTY).

16. after you get out of the detestable ditch of... DISLIKE, (DISDAIN & DESPITE).

17. after you get out of the derelict ditch of... DEFIANCE, (DISOBEDIENCE & DELINQUENCY).

18. after you get out of the dismal ditch of... DOGGED DISQUIET, (DEJECTION & DESPERATION).

19. after you get out of the defamatory ditch of... DISCREDIT, (DISGRACE & DISHONOR).

20. after you get out of the decrying ditch of... DISCOURTESY, (DISPRAISE & DISESTEEM).

21. after you get out of the despoiling ditch of... DERANGEMENT, (DISCOMFITURE & DISORIENTATION).

22. after you get out of the downtrodden ditch of... DAMPNESS, (DISCONTENT & DISAPPOINTMENT).

23. after you get out of the dissident ditch of... DISENCHANTMENT, (DISAPPROVAL & DISCOMMENDATION).

24. after you get out of the disaffiliated ditch of... DISASSOCIATION, (DISCONNECTION & DISSOLUTION).

25. after you get out of the discriminative ditch of... DEMARCATION, (DIFFERENTIATION & DISSEVERATION).

26. after you get out of the decremental ditch of... DILUTION, (DISSECTION & DIMINUTION).

27. after you get out of the dunderpate ditch of... DIMNESS, (DULLNESS & DUMBNESS).

28. after you get out of the desolate ditch of DESPOLIATION, (DESTRUCTION & DISASTER).

29. after you get out of the debunking ditch of... DEPRECIATION, (DEFLATION & DEROGATION).

30. after you get out of the dominative ditch of... DOMINION, (DICTATORSHIP & DESPOTISM).

31. after you get out of the demigodkin ditch of... DAEMONS, (DEMIGODS & DEMAGOGUES).

32. after you get out of the dearful ditch of... DARLINGS, (DESCENDANTS & DYNASTIES).

33. after you get out of the disputative ditch of... DEBATE, (DIATRIBE & DISCEPTATION).

34. after you get out of the daunting ditch of... DISADVANTAGE, (DISCOMMODITY & DEPRIVATION).

35. after you get out of the disconsolate ditch of... DISPOSSESSION, (DERELECTION & DISHERISON).

36. after you get out of the disabused ditch of... DESISTANCE, (DEFECTION & DESERTION).

37. after you get out of the desultory ditch of... DESPONDENCY, (DEPRESSION & DISPAIR).

38. after you get out of the deplorable ditch of... DISSIPATION, (DISPOSITION & DESTITUTION).

39. after you get out of the deleterious ditch of... DENOUNCEMENT, (DENUNCIATION & DENIGRATION).

40. after you get out of the drudging ditch of... (DUTIFUL) DEVOTION, (DEPENDENCY & DEADLOCK).

41. after you get out of the dumpish ditch of... DOWNCASTNESS, (DISPIRITEDNESS & DOWNHEARTEDNESS).

42. after you get out of the demoralizing ditch of... DEGRADATION, (DEGENERACY & DEPRAVATION).

43. after you get out of the determinate ditch of... DOCTRINE, (DOGMA & DENOMINATION).

44. after you get out of the disclaiming ditch of... DENIAL, (DISAVOWAL & DISOWNMENT).

45. after you get out of the delineatory ditch of... DEFINITION, (DELIMITATION & DETERMINATION).

46. after you get out of the dugout ditch of... DISSENT, (DEFENCE & DOORKEEPING).

47. after you get out of the delatorian ditch of... DEPRECATION, (DEFAMATION & DEFILEMENT).

48. after you get out of the disreputable ditch of... DEMORALIZATION, (DEFLORATION & DESECRATION).
49. after you get out of the disheartening ditch of... DEFEAT, (DEFAULT & DOWNFALL).
50. after you get out of the decaying ditch of... DEGENERATION, (DILAPIDATION & DISREPAIR).
51. after you get out of the dissuasive ditch of... DEFICIENCY, (DELAY & DRAWBACK).
52. after you get out of the disseminating ditch of... DRUMBEATING, (DECLAMATION & DEMONSTRATION).
53. after you get out of the drazzmatazzing ditch of... DAZZLE, (DAZE & DISPLAY).
54. after you get out of the demotivating ditch of... DETERMENT, (DETRIMENT & DEFERMENT).
55. after you get out of the damnatory ditch of... DEBASEMENT, (DEBAUCHERY & DECADENCE).
56. after you get out of the dizzying ditch of... DAPPERLY DRESSED, (DERRING-DO & DEBUTANT).
57. after you get out of the dilatory ditch of... DILLYDALLYING, (DAWDLING & DABBLING).
58. after you get out of the draggletailed ditch of... DISARRANGEMENT, (DISHEVELMENT & DISCOMPOSURE).
59. after you get out of the dronish ditch of... DULLARD, (DOLT AND DUNCE).
60. after you get out of the debilitating ditch of... DEADNESS, (DEADHEADEDNESS & DEAD-ENDEDNESS).

61. after you get out of the distancing ditch of... DISENGAGEMENT, (DEADPAN DETACHMENT & DESENSITIZED DECENTRALIZATION).

62. after you get out of the dyadic ditch of... DOUBLETONS, (DOUBLE-DUTCH & DISPOSABLE DUETS).

63. after you get out of the doldrum ditch of... DONNISM, (DITTO & DATA).

64. after you get out of the domestic ditch of... DUTY, (DEVOIR & DYSPEPSIA).

65. after you get out of the dreary ditch of... DEADLINES, (DELIVERY & DUES).

66. after you get out of the dubiously-dignifying ditch of... DECOR, (DECKING & DECORUM).

67. after you get out of the deferentially-divisive ditch of... DIVINITY, (DONATISM & DIVINATION).

68. after you get out of the dually-didymous ditch of... DAYLIGHT & DARKNESS, (DEVILTRY & DEITY, DELIVERANCE & DAMNATION).

69. after you get out of the disingenous ditch of... DASHING DEDICATION, (DISGUISED DEVOTEDNESS & DEADPAN DIARRHEA).

70. after you get out of the derogative ditch of...DEMOTION, (DEFROCKING & DEPORTMENT).

71. after you get out of the distillatory ditch of... (DEAR) DIONYSUS, (DEEP DRINKING & DEAD DRUNK-ENNESS).

72. after you get out of the drumming-down ditch of... DETAINMENT, (DETENTION & (the) DREADFUL DUNGEON).

73. after you get out of the depletive ditch of... DREARINESS, (DROOPINESS & DORMANCY).

74. after you get out of the demimonde ditch of... DRESS, (DOLLS & DRAG).

75. after you get out of the downrushing ditch of... DOPE, (DRUGS & DEALINGS).

76. after you get out of the dramaturgic ditch of... DRAMA, (DAFTNESS & DIORAMA).

77. after you get out of the diametrical ditch of... DUALISM, (DUALITY & DICHOTOMY).

78. after you get out of the dingdong ditch of... DRUDGERY, (DOGGEDNESS & DUPLICATION).

79. after you get out of the deviatory ditch of... DEFLEXION, (DIVARICATION & DIVAGATION).

80. after you get out of the declivitous ditch of... DECLENSION, (DEBACLE & DOOM).

81. after you get out of the doddering ditch of... DISSOCIATION, (DISINTEGRATION & DEMENTIA).

82. after you get out of the decorous ditch of... DOCILITY, (DELICACY & DECENCY).

83. after you get out of the dissonant ditch of... DISHARMONY, (DISCORDANCE & DISACCORD).

84. after you get out of the dashed ditch of... DOLEFULNESS, (DOURNESS & DOWNS).

85. after you get out of the dismaying ditch of... DYSTHYMIA, (DIPSOMANIA & DELIRIUM).

86. after you get out of the dank and darkened ditch of... DIRK, (DAGGER & DOUBLE-CROSS).

87. after you get out of the downhill ditch of... DECREMENT, (DECREASE & DEPLETION).

88. after you get out of the disruptive ditch of... DEPREDATION, (DEVASTATION & DECIMATION).

89. after you get out of the distasteful ditch of... DISAPPROBATION, (DISCLAMATION & DISMISSAL).

90. after you get out of the daredevil ditch of... DARINGNESS, (DOUGHTINESS & DAMSEL DELIVERANCE).

91. after you get out of the denaturing ditch of... DEFLOWERMENT, (DEVOLUTION & DEPRAVITY).

92. after you get out of the disabling ditch of... DEBT, (DUENESS & DENUDATION).

93. after you get out of the downward-dipping ditch of... DESCENT, (DECELERATION & DECRESCENDO).

94. after you get out of the demeaning ditch of... DETRACTION, (DISFAVOR & DISCREDITATION).

95. after you get out of the discommending ditch of... DERISIVE DISCOURSE, (DEVIOUS DELIBERATION & DASTARDLY DEED).

96. after you get out of the discoloring ditch of... DISTINGUISHMENT, (DENOTATION & DIFFERENTIA).

97. after you get out of the disincentive ditch of... DISTRESS, (DIFFICULTY & DISPLEASURE).

98. after you get out of the desperado ditch of... DESOLATENESS, (DESTITUTENESS & DISGRACEFULNESS).

99. after you get out of the driveling, drooling, and dreaded ditch of... DOPPELGÄNGERS, (DRAGONS & DRACULAS).

100. after you get out of the Dorje-drawn ditch of... (DEVELOPMENTAL) DISEASE, (DENOUEMENT, DEPARTURE, DEATH & DECOMPOSITION).

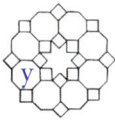

The True when *judged* stand Still inside, and Love.
The True when *praised* stand Still inside, and Love.

The True when *loved* stand Still inside, and *Liquefy*.

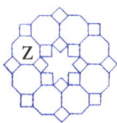

Push and pull another and you be powerful, man!
Push and pull yourself and you be Masterful... *Oh my* SOUL!

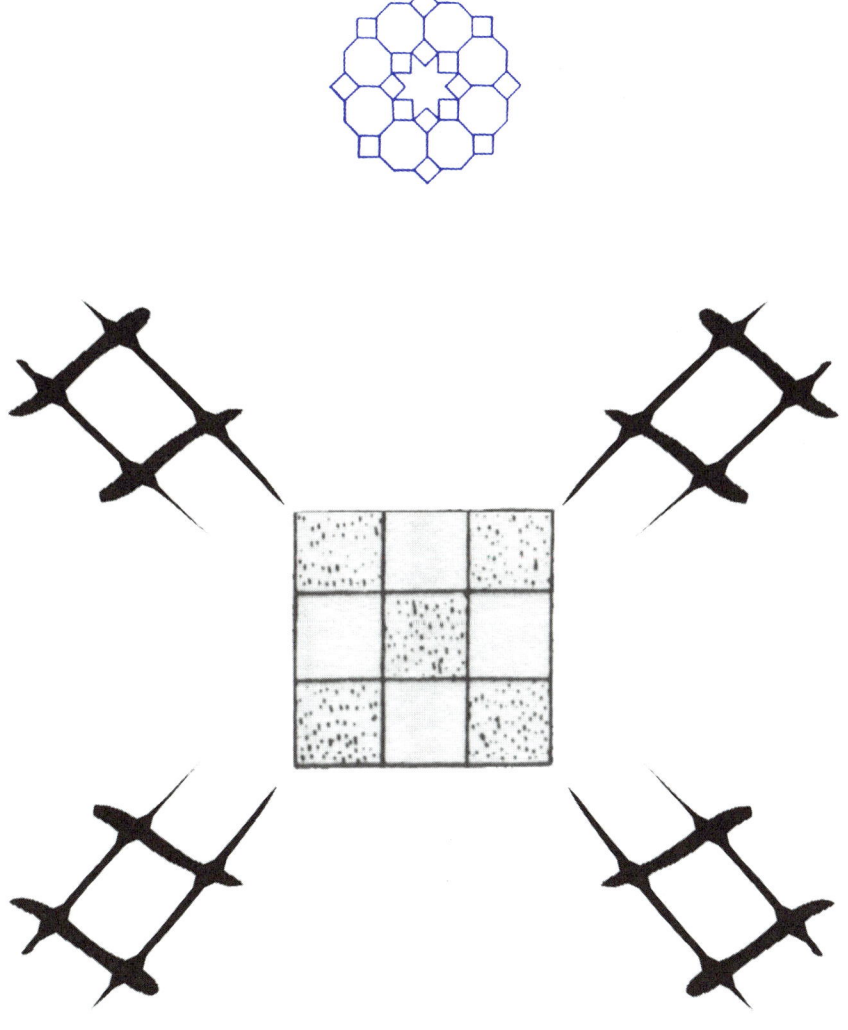

Bubble Gum & Betty Boopers

X

Knots of Eternity

Paradoxes from Dadi to Daughter

Bubble Gum & Betty Boopers

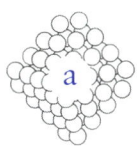

Better by gum to blazon a benevolent listen to your blunders, blotches and bloopers than to habitually, blindly, and brazenly brush off the blatant befooleries of the ego.

Better by gum to bypass the braying boo-boos of the 'I' by benightedly banking-off and burying the self under some bright, bodacious blanket of 'ben brio' behavior; or, by the bardy bones of Big Bird, brashly brandishing the bored bâton of the bohemian self to the breathless bewitchment of a blinkin' balmy brainchild, or if the bloody ball bounces at a bevel, then some banzai busy-ness.

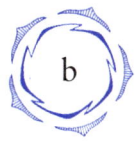

Better by gum a test failed in the service of the Good, than a test carried off, (or triumphed in), through the agency of the Bad.

Better by gum to be a Wise nobody than some silly someone, (with a significant *name*).

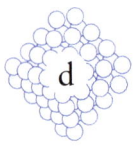

Better by gum to greet the good and the Godliness in everyone, rather than the bad and the worldliness in all... (even if lately, it is the latter condition which seems to be appallingly apparent).

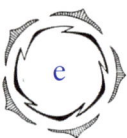

Better by gum to gaze at garlanded Kim and to gallantly grin; than to gawk at gorgeous Joan and to gag on a hoary groan.

Better by gum to gaze at Bettie-Lee with a genuine glee and a gathering gladness; than to gawk at Betty-Bop with the gilded glowings of a gigolo and the grinning gonads of a goat.

Better by gum to get to know the *ego-self* and to become its sympathetic friend; than to ignore it and be forced before long, to face an unsympathetic foe.

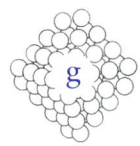

Better by gum to chew harder on the (black) Bubblegum of a 'wanton narcissism', than to bequeath any lasting happiness to the gladdening gratification of a mere passing passion.

Better by gum to chew harder on the (pink) Bubblegum of a 'selfish significance', than dare to posit forth an impotent and temporary peace, as being permutable with the 'POW!' of Real Relief.

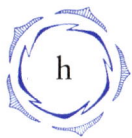

Better by gum to deal with the addiction than to mate with the Nightmare.

Better by gum to let the anger go than to let the Hatred grow.

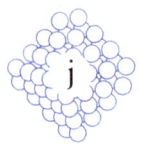

Better by gum to experience, know and become the 'J<small>OY</small> of the Whole Show', than to live for the prurient pursuit of *mere* pleasure, or for the *easy* and *able* sidestepping of pain.

Better by gum to turn numb than to play dumb: numbness at least, is Genuine.

Better by gum to sow serenity and bestow Bliss, and to thereby Bless as you walk, eat and sleep, than to buzz about 'blissed-out', and think yourself Blessed.

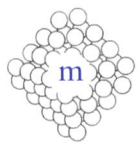

Better by gum to play a goodly and Godly 'plain-Jane', than to set-up on stage the avaricious subterfuge of an 'ego-self', in the foolhardy role of a sanctimonious Saint James.

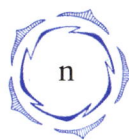

Better by gum to practice the uncommon ceremony and joyful celebration of breaking 'Sacred Ground' in this HERE place, *mindfully*, in full conscious awareness and heightened tempo, to our CREATOR's karmic memo.

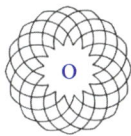

Better by gum for your Being to be on the bum, than (forever) on the run.

Better by gum to dance on the dark dot, than to dash dauntlessly from the dingy dot, and dart desperately to Dartmouth.

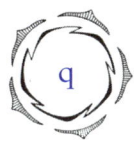

Better by gum (to learn) to brush your teeth while upside-down, than to slosh (about) in self-pity, while right-side up.

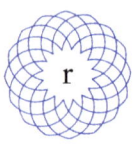

Better by gum to Love the face in front of you, not because she smiled, but because the Smile of Existence, (just) happened to find her Face.

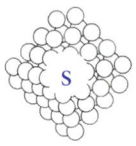

Better by gum to be sincerely sad, than to be deviously glad.

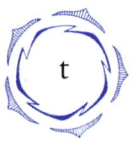

Better by gum to take-in the 'Whole of It All', willingly and with jubilation, rather than to reject out of hand, even a particle part.

Better by gum, to take-in the 'Whole of the Part', spontaneously and with exultation, than to reject out of careless slight, even a poor particle.

Better by gum to Love all and to like a few a little less.

Better (still), by gum to like all and to Love the infamous few you don't, even more.

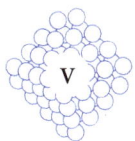

Better by gum to get bopped good on the sorry beeper and to let all resentment and embitteredness bleed in liberating blotches upon a contrite breast; than to continue to hoard-up sour lemons and to imbibe the hot wine of blame, bitterly-enclosed, within a boiling bladder of grim unpardon.

Better by gum to Self-ishly will the Divine into one's sadhana and do selflessly what the Divine Wills… than to insist upon piling-up a piffling sense of 'self-will' in one's daily life, even if it all seems… so 'selfishly-right'.

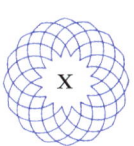

Better by gum to give credence to the dream of self-destiny and to just go ahead and devour life as it *apparently* seems to be, than to believe it is *real*.

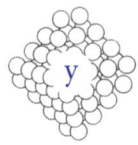

Better by gum to apperceive A.S.A.P. that the present moment surreptitiously slips into the slipper of the past more quickly than the mind can possibly comprehend, but... "Ahh, the *comely Comfort!*"

Better by gum to reverently reflect and to everywhere genuinely Genuflect, than to be hopelessly heedless and end up in a hollow heap... impishly headless, and sadly Unhallowed.

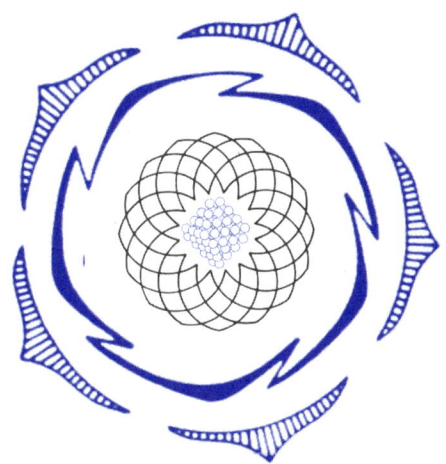

Blinkins'

XI

Knots of Eternity

Paradoxes from Dadi to Daughter

Blinkins'

The Master says: "You be your Self, I'll be your TAXI".

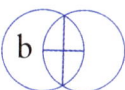

To run after an answer is to court the Lie.

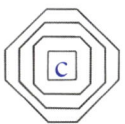

Intuit the TRUTH, then explore the Logic.

If it grabs your attention, it's interesting!
If it doesn't, GOD is boring you to 'Wakefulness'.

Blinkins'

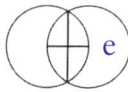

When dank darkness descends, the Bright beckons.

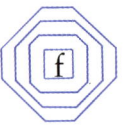

"Hey Mamma, if I munch on Manna, will I leaven into Life?"

Love GOD today, and be *satiated* tomorrow.

Love GOD Now, and kiss the next second goodbye.

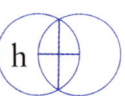

The Master may have revealed my SELF, but the Self done begat *me* first, before *aham* got around to identify It.

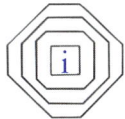

Please find your way to Me; then promptly get Lost.

If you take care of Time, then each ticking second, will take Care of you.

We kabong upon the *base drum* but we 'bam bam' upon the *tam-tam*.

We knock upon the *kettledrum* but we 'go congo' upon the *bongos*.

We beat bombastically upon *Big Boy*, but we bonk blindly upon the *Small Fry*.

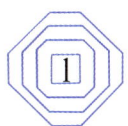

Do not pester the Teacher like a pup; but do *hound* his Teachings.

There is really only one thing as good as Nothing: 'EVERYTHING'.

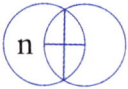

The path to GREAT EQUANIMITY is the way of the 'Great White Sweat'.

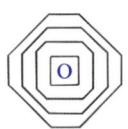

"Not at all, not at all, well blow me down!"

"I knew GOD not at all!"

Get out of my meditation Wanda, your boobs are making my mind bob!

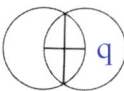

The karmic legacy of a hellish hate bespeaks of a *scarred psyche* in horrid escape and a *seared self* in hot pursuit.

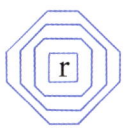

Light destroys the darkness of the mind;
Love disbands the dazzle of desire.

Light deactivates the delusions of the id;
Love dismantles the caparison of passion.

Honest with yourself, honest with the world.

Kind to yourself, kind to all.

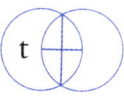

Barely are we a blink of an 'I' away from being blinkin' blind, or blinkin' Bright.

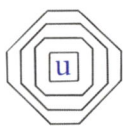

"The sun rises, be at Peace."
"The sun sets, rest in Peace."

To be at peace with your pleasure is to enjoy the earth's treasure.
To rest in peace with your pain is to enjoy the earth's rain.

Everything is a dream, a dream, a Dream!

Is that why you snort the coke of experience, and then turn around and snore so loudly in Life's conscious sleep?

The Basic Self is complete and already plentiful.

All else is mere addition and addiction.

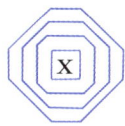

The Raw Material of Life is literally *the all of life*.

The sadhaka must therefore, always remain *mindful and vigilant*.

Spiritually-speaking, just about anything, *ordinary or corny*, could actually be the real 'Wake-up Call'!

Divinely lambent becomes the Lover of GOD whose heart of gold has been worldly-burnished, lovingly-broken, blissfully-burned, and heavenly-buried.

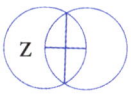

Corked and cocked with consecrated choler Chuck barehandedly chucks a coalescent chunk of charcoal at wicked Chris and in a quick karmic crackle the poor peccable prodigal permutes instantly into a sizzling 'charcoaled chuckroast' for the Sainted Table.

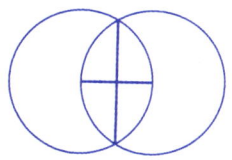

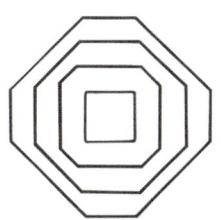

Divine Ascriptions

XII

Knots of Eternity
Paradoxes from Dadi to Daughter

Divine Ascriptions

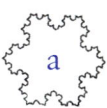

Because you fell, He picked you up.

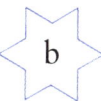

Because you became as naught, He made you into all men.

Because you knocked, He came to the door.

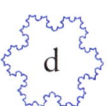

Because you were sorry, He turned over the page.

Divine Ascriptions

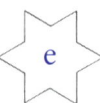

Because you vanished, He placed you Everywhere.

Because you forgave, He took your hand.

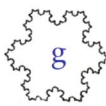

Because you stayed ordinary, He knighted you Extraordinary.

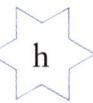

Because you had respect, He Dignified you.

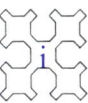

Because you gave space, He lent a Wing to your Horizon.

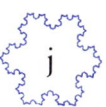

Because you became a child, He endowed you with Innocence.

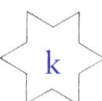

Because you nurtured another, He sent you the Mother.

Because you cared to care, He awakened Compassion.

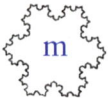

Because you sanctified your Self, He Blessed you.

Because you celebrated the world, He Celebrated you.

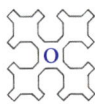

Because you braved the dark, He Lighted you.

Because you blew yourself out, He bowed before the Emptiness.

Because you had conscience, He showed you Consciousness.

Because you Burned, He Lit (for you) the Heavens.

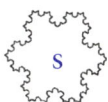

Because you questioned, He Answered the answer.

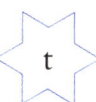

Because you kept your word, He left His Word with you.

Because you stuck to sadhana, He Spiritualized you.

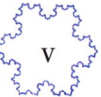

Because you wearied and fainted not, He gave you more Work.

Because you doubted and dropped not, He gave you more trials and tests.

Because you had Faith, He gave you His Force.

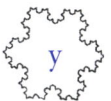

Because you took Him as yours, He Possessed you.

Because you did without doing, He did Everything Effortlessly.

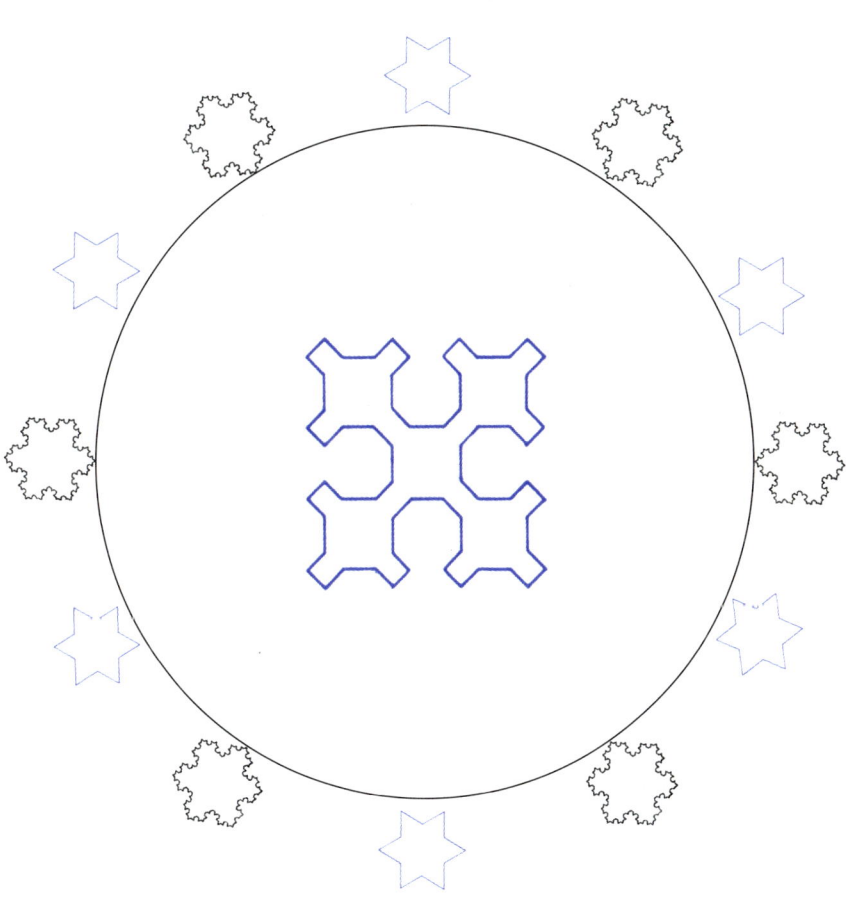

Inspired Imputations

XIII

Knots of Eternity

Paradoxes from Dadi to Daughter

Inspired Imputations

Because you yearned (for) the Answer, He handed you the Question.

Because you had Hunger, He quenched your Thirst, (first).

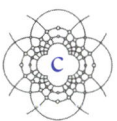

Because you Cried out in ignorance, He consoled you into Wisdom.

Because you sought to Understand, He Entered you from all sides.

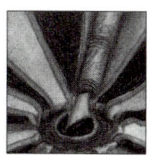

Inspired Imputations

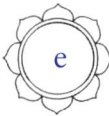

Because you strove to Hear, He blew on His Hornpipes, Silently.

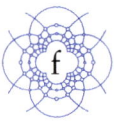

Because you engrossed your mind with Only Him, He Meditated you.

Because you learned with difficulty, He took (Humble) root in your Teacher.

Because you became old in Him, He became Forever Young in you.

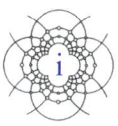

Because you made 'muni muni', He blasted you with 'Tutti Frutti'.

Because you were lost, He sent out a Search party.

Because you wore a beard, He Shaved you.

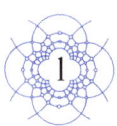

Because you honed your Heart, He Hummed and Hummed.

Because you loved Him, He Loved you first.

Because you sank into Stillness, He (Sweetly) transmitted the Truth.

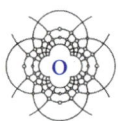

Because you became a cell of God, He became the All of you.

Because you (often) deployed your dot, He had a hard time being Caught.

Because you stopped going to church, He Came to your Heart, (to Sit).

Because you did all for Him, He Did It to you long Before.

Because you discovered Infinity, He became finite.

Because you opened your Eye, He saw Himself.

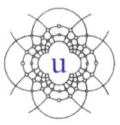

Because you aimed for God, He scrunched Himself up into the Target.

Because you caused your ego-egg to crack, He was able to Spill-in.

Because you sacrificed yourself, He Crucified you.

Because you became broken, He broke up Heaven upon an Angel's back.

Because you climbed up one side of the Mountain, He Happily slid down the other side, (with you).

Because you (so) loved to dance in a circle, He Waited, and Rested right in the Middle.

Rusty Hinges

XIV

Knots of Eternity
Paradoxes from Dadi to Daughter

Rusty Hinges

Are you censuring the world, or is the world denouncing you?
Are you criticizing people, or are people declaiming you?

Even as you judge, people mark you; as you criticize, *le monde* measures you; as you censure, the world evaluates you.

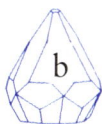

Superior it is to see the Sacred today and extolling it, pass away... than to live till tomorrow, and die cursing in the devil's den.

Learn to expend yourself superiorly today, without reserve, in matters great and small, and Mother Perfection will one day stop by your essence station, and fill Herself up with the octane of GODLY GOLD.

Rusty Hinges

Do it, do it, do it, and live Life *now* as She offers Herself to you... upon the passing moment of challenge and present desire.

Do it, do it, do it, or the Great Gobbledygook will gobble you up... because you shied away, stayed chicken, or played dead.

Upon the grinching of rusty human hinges rests the Harmony of the Spheres.

Being much Empty governs the art of doing much Muchly.

There is no pilgrim upon the Path without the *pilgrimage*.

Without the *Journey*, endings are mere mirages, mousetraps, and husks of emptiness: that is to say, *terminals do not amount to tiddles without the Trip.*

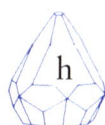

Drop by drop, the good Master fills your vessel with Emptiness, till your Bucket of Life overspills with Grace, and each and every experience of the day is drenched in Shakti-Gold.

A boorish bag of bad bones betokens bedevilment, bathos, and bedlam in the Basilica.

Sometime later, much much later upon the Dharma Path, you boldly drop away from the Space-Time continuum, and you pop-up *radically surprised* as the Inherent SELF... a very Omniscient Cell, somewhere-Everywhere and precisely-Nowhere, upon GOD's *Episcopal Epiglottis*.

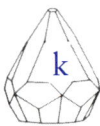

To walk the Secret Way, you must untie the Gordian Knot of *Egoji,* and die in absolute *Wakefulness* on the spot!

To lead strongly you must follow humbly.
To decide justly, you must love perfectly.

To know rightly, you must understand correctly.
To act potently, you must accomplish wisely.

To speak uprightly, you must integrate the enemy.
To inspire greatly, you must exemplify (life) passionately.

To communicate unerringly, you must have *a priori* communed, with the very depths of (your) Emptiness.

Do good once and you'll like it; do good twice and you'll savor it; do good thrice, and it will nevermore suffice.

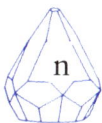

The stately subduing of the stark, selfish self is spiritually superior to the strong samurai who steely slays a slew of sinewy soldiers, single-handedly.

Prolong pretense, provision and pretext, and you but protract the pure pardon of your prodigality.

For *aspirants*: "Inside is the Soul, outside is your *suffering*."
For *disciples*: "Inside is the Self, outside is your *mission*."
For *initiates*: "Inside is Pure Essence, outside is your *Emptiness*."

The promotion of pride predisposes the Pilgrim to perdition.

The honing of humility wafts the Wind of Wisdom into the Wayfarer's world.

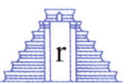

To become calm and clear upon encountering Lord Kwannon eclipses all forms of knowledge and erudition.

Trust *not*, and you Achieve not.
Trust *little*, and you Attain little.
Trust *much*, and you Accomplish much.

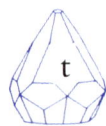

To recognize an Awakened Man and to '*swaha-bow*' to him with a ready respect and a full alertness, is superior to a thousand kowtows and honorings of stale buddha statues.

To behold the Truth presently *present* in the palm of broad Buddha-daylight, beats the holing-up of the self for a hundred years in a musty monastery, murmuring mantras, munching over scriptures, and mulling over Emptiness... in some untold thousands of predictable, empty-minded meditations.

An episodic memory of spiritual hype means absolutely nothing, if its sacred tale betrays the tiniest tinge, or twist, of an ass' tail.

To untimely seek out a Sage to solve your stresses and take you out of dire straits, is somewhat like shooting for the Polestar, and landing in a sea of Spiritual scotch.

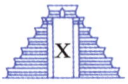

Delusional pretense to authentic Spirituality satisfies no one but the sincere hypocrite.

It is so sad to see so many seekers converge upon a genuine Master prematurely and unprepared, and to sorely importune and indiscriminately impose their aspirations and presumptions, and penchants and impurities... upon Him.

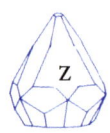

Although you can never be 'ready enough' to meet a True Teacher, you can at least prime yourself to lay down the groundwork, or leastways, do the necessary non-stop practice, to *Be Prepared*.

Glossary

Adi Shiva: Primal Shiva, third member of the Hindu Trinity known as the Lord of Destruction.

Aham: The subjective sense of "I am"; the "I exist".

Ahamkara: "I" as the always conditional ego; the pride of existence; egoism; vanity.

Ahimsa: The principle of non-violence; harmlessness; the five restraints and five moral observances.

Ananda: Bliss from the heart, Joy from the mind, Ecstasy from the body... all identifying with the Self.

Ashram: (from the sanskrit word "Shrama", *effort*); a center for spiritual studies and meditation, usually under the guidance of an Instructor, a Master or Guru.

Atma: The Divine Soul.

Atman: The Transcendental Self.

Avatar: A physical incarnation of the Divine Consciousness.

Baba-ji: The planet earth's "Mahavatar", (Great Avatar); deathless, he physically lives in the Himalayas, but His Omni-Presence bestows a guidance and constant blessing on the world, (and world events).

Baraka (Barakat): A blessing, grace, or gift of definite Divine benediction coming from a place, object, or person of holiness.

Bodhi: The state of Awakening or Illumination (leading to Liberation).

Bodhi Tree: The sacred tree under which the Buddha awakened and was Enlightened.

Bodhichitta: The Awakened mind; the mind of Enlightenment which manifests in compassion.

Bodhisattva: A Realized Buddha who has made a vow of service to all sentient beings, sacrificing his own immediate and complete liberation, to compassionately aid and uplift mankind.

Brahman: The Ultimate Reality; the Absolute; the Transcendental Self.

Budh: Budh or Buddh, being the root syllable for Bodhi, meaning 'awake'; therefore, by implication, the 'Awakened One', and thusly, a Buddha.

Buddhi: The Wisdom faculty; Higher Mind; Soul-ar Intuition; Pure Reason; Gnosis.

Chaitanya: Bhakti, Devotional Bliss; Ecstatic Consciousness; Great Bengali (Vaishnava) Saint of the 15-16th century, whose devotional passion for Krishna became legend.

Chenrezi: "Looking with clear eyes"; the Tibetan form of Avalokiteshvara, the Bodhisattva of Compassion.

Da: "The One Who Gives"; the Divine Giver of Inherent Heart, (or Love) Bliss.

Dadi: The God Giver of Grace; the Servant of Self and the Slave of Spirit; the dynamic *Father Principle* and gentle *Feminine Force* joined in Name.

Dharma: Divine Duty; daily right action; the Way (of Truth); Law of the Spirit.

Dharmakaya: Doctrine of the teachings of Buddha; the true nature of the Buddha which is identical with Absolute Reality; the essence of the universe; the transcendental space of Being.

Dharmata: The innate nature of Dharma, the fundamental Essence that is the clear basis of everything.

Diksha: Initiation; the transmission of wisdom (jnana), and the transfer of power (shakti), from Master to disciple.

Dokhma: A pit surrounded by a low stone tower with a grated top on which the Parsees place their dead.

Dhyana: Meditation or contemplation; the state of deep Stillness and inner Poise reached in advanced stages of meditation.

Green Tara: Embodies the 'active compassion' aspect of all Buddhas; the female Buddha of enlightened activity; she is said to have emanated from the tears of the left eye of Bodhisattva AVALOKETISHWARA, in order to aid Him in his great Compassionate Work; she also helps to remove obstacles and serves as a potent protector of her devotees.

Guru: Spiritual Teacher/Preceptor/Instructor/Guide/Master; one who is mature, ripe, or "heavy with the fruit" of Wisdom.

Hanuman: Hindu divinity representing the perfect disciple, who manifested in the form of a monkey; the devoted servant of Rama, his Lord.

Hara: A name for Shiva, representing the fire/heat of disintegration and destruction; the dispeller of darkness and ignorance.

Hari: The 'consoler'/'comforter'; the Divine Robber who removes, or steals, from the heart of his devotee, the negative conditions related to ignorance, sin and sorrow; one of the many forms of Vishnu.

Hridaya(m): The True Heart; the Heart of Hearts; the Cave of the Heart.

Hum: A sacred mantric syllable representing/facilitating the wisdom Mind of the Buddhas.

Indra: The Lord of the heavens; Hindu God of thunder/lightning symbolizing spiritual power and the flash, (or flashes), of Illumination.

Ishwara (Ishvara): Creator of the universe; the personification of the Absolute; Lord of the Manifest; the 'Lord' within man; a personalized, venerated form of the Lord.

Japa: A constant and rapid repetition of the Lord's name; the practice of mantra.

Ji: An adjunctive syllable given to a name as a sign of honoring and respect.

Jivatma: The incarnated Soul; the individualized, human Soul.

Jnana-Marg: The Path of Knowledge; the Way of Wisdom.

Kama: The Creative Principle; the Primal Impulse behind the desire of Existence to exist; also, often used in relation to passion, affection and (all the delights of) desire.

Karma: Law of cause and effect; action and reaction; 'as you sow, so shall you reap'.

Kaya(s): Body or vehicle of manifestation; various dimensions and manifestations of an enlightened being.

Krishna: An avatar who lived in India three millenniums before the Christian era and whose divine counsel to Arjuna, (who symbolizes the incarnated Soul), in the Bhagavad Gita, is revered by countless God-seekers; the Indian counterpart to Christ (Consciousness).

Krupa: Divine Grace emanating from the Guru.

Kwannon: Avalokiteshvara, Mahakaruna Buddha, the Buddha of Great Compassion; also known in Japan as Kannon or Kanzeon, in China as Kuan Yin, and in Tibet as Chenrezi.

Leela, (or Lila): A divine play, or action of the Lord vis-à-vis His Creation.

Linga(m): The male mark, sign, or symbol of Shiva; it represents the Fundamental Form, Primordial Power, or Pure Consciousness which cannot be destroyed by death, or by any other means; it also stands for the undying subtle body, the indivisible Monad, and Divinity Unclothed.

Lokesvara: A four-armed manifestation of Avalokiteshwara, the Bodhisattva of Compassion.

Mahakali: The Great Kali, a form of Shakti, as the embodiment of the Force of Destruction; also as Divine Wisdom which puts an end to all illusion; the Black One, the slayer of demons and the unreal.

Mahanam: The practice of the recitation of the Name of God; chanting the Great Name of the Supreme Lord.

Mahatma: A great Soul/Self in selfless service to the greater enlightenment of Humanity.

Mandir: Literally "abode of God"; home of a Deity; a temple honoring a Divinity, or housing the Divine.

Manjushri: Bodhisattva of Great Wisdom; in Tibetan Buddhism Manjushri embodies the incisive wisdom that dispels the darkness of ignorance.

Manna: Grace from heaven; the descent of Divine inspiration; a form of spiritual food giving self a sense of empowerment.

Mantra(m): Potent recitations, incantations and invocations made-up of sanskrit seed syllables and the names of Lords.

Mara: The incarnation of the Negative Force in Buddhism; it also symbolizes the desires and passions which enslave man, as well as those obstacles which may impede his progress towards enlightenment.

Maya: Illusion; relative phantom-existence; the created universe as being a play of illusion, and giving rise to false knowledge, untruth, and ignorance; the Veil which hides the Vision (of Truth).

Metanoia: A radical reorientation of the self being repolarized to the Self; a profound inner movement and repositioning of one's whole being through the surrender or relinquishment of the ego's normal hold on existence; a metamorphic modification, a transformative turnabout, or a total transfiguration.

Monad: The indivisible primordial Self; Spirit Essence; the Divine Womb or Primordial Matrix giving birth to a collectivity of Souls.

Muni: The science of abiding in inner Silence; an ascetic whose sadhana is Silence.

Nabhikalpa, Navikalpa Samadhi: A state of perfect samadhi; *absolute* tranquil abiding at the Center of the Self, where eventually, the seeds of all previous samskaras, (subconscious patterns, or vibrational impressions), are completely burnt, or neutralized.

Nadis: A network of subtle or energy channels of which the etheric body is composed.

Nirvana: A state of High Enlightenment, where true Liberation is released and Integral Oneness lived.

Nish-Karma (Naishkarmya Karman): Similar to Wei Wu Wei... that is, *actionless action*, *effortless effort*; therefore, action, thought or emotion which has no karmic repercussions.

Om: The Spiritual sound of Creation; the Word (gone forth); the Verb; the Primordial Vibration which sustains all worlds.

Om Mani Padme Hum: lit. 'Om, Jewel in the Lotus (of the Heart), Hum'; a well known mantra in Tibetan Buddhism; the compassion mantra associated with Avalokiteshwara.

Om Tat Sat: "I Am the Truth which Is the very Essence of Om"; "I Am That".

Padmakara: 'Lotus Born', a synonym for Padmasambhava, or Guru Rinpoche.

Padmapani: Known as the "Lotus-Bearer"; one of the more common epithets of Avalokiteshvara, the Bodhisattva of Infinite Compassion.

Para Param Purusha: The Supreme High Lord; the Highest of the High; the God of Gods.

Prajna: Knowledge qualified by the Highest Consciousness; Universal-type Wisdom.

Prajnaparamita: The Goddess of transcendental wisdom; the wisdom of all buddhas personified in the enlightened form of a female deity. The *Prajnaparamita-Sutra* is regarded as the holy mother that feeds the bodhisattva with the amrita (nectar) of prajna (transcendental wisdom), and guides him to *paramita* (the other shore).

Pranaam: Profound salutation and humble obeisance.

Prarabdha (Pralabdha): The inevitable, present life destiny which is in accordance with our past karma; and whose influence, in the best of possible worlds, should be met with an open consciousness, and worked through.

Prasad: A blessed or divine gift; often refers to food that has been offered to God, and is thus blessed by Him through the intercession of a Guru, Saint, Priest or Holy Person.

Prashchit: True repentance as part of the process of Purification.

Prema: Love of God; Love of Self; and Divine Love for all of creation.

Puja: Ritual worship in which a deity is invoked in the form of an idol, or picture, and is propitiated as a Divine guest with offerings of flowers, fruits and other eatables, along with the recitation of appropriate mantras and an expression of relevant signs.

Purusha: The Primordial Lord; the Animating, or Primeval Male Principle in man; the "Creative Collectivity" of Creation; the Creative Cognized Self as Pure Spirit (male), as distinguished from Prakiti (feminine creative energy, matter, maya).

Pu'Tai (Bu'Tai), Ch'i-tzu: A wandering, wonder-working, miracle-making monk said to have lived in 10th century China; in all Chinese monasteries he is represented as the laughing Buddha; he was a lover and creator of many *paradoxes* of Ch'an, (or Zen), Buddhism; only at the time of his death did he reveal his true identity as an incarnation of the future Buddha MAITREYA.

Rama: The seventh Avatar, an incarnation of Vishnu and the hero of the Ramayana.

Roshi: In Zen, the venerable Master.

Sabhikalpa, Savikalpa Samadhi: A state of *temporary*, Spiritual Stillness and Absorption, in which the seeds of previous karma continue to exist.

Sadhak(a): Spiritual aspirant/student; a disciple; a shishya; a chela.

Sadhana : Spiritual discipline and practice; the duties of Discipleship.

Saddhu, Sadh: A wandering spiritual mendicant; a holy man, a saint; one who has attained siddhis (powers), through asceticism and intensely sustained effort.

Saiemoud : A sacred appellation of God; GOD, the Absolute; the LIFE of the Central Sun.

Samantabhadra: "He Who Is All-Pervading and All-Good", or "He Whose Beneficient Goodness Is Everywhere"; also known as Vajradhara; the ultimate Primordial Buddha, or Adi Buddha; one of the most significant Buddhas of Mahayana Buddhism and Dzogchen.

Samayas: Vows of engagement taken towards the Master and his lineage; a sacred pledge to follow the Dharma and uphold the spiritual path.

Samboghakaya: One of the three bodies of the Buddha; the body of Bliss or the enjoyment body; 'timeless ecstatic communication', without beginning or without end.

Samsara: The wheel of rebirth, the process of worldly life; the cycle of rebirths that a being goes through within the various modes of existence until final liberation is attained.

Sangha: A Buddhist community or brotherhood; in common usage, a confrererie or comradeship of similar Souls upon a spiritual Path.

Saraswati: The Hindu Mother Goddess embodying the *creative spirit* of all fine arts; She is the active Essence, or Consort of Brahma.

Sat Chit Ananda: Existence, Knowledge, Bliss.

Satguru: A spiritual Teacher of Truth.

Satsang, Sat-sangha: A meeting of devotees; "the company of Truth"; being associated with the presence of Sadhs, (Sadhus), Siddhas (perfected Adepts), and Self-Realized Masters.

Sensei: Honorable Teacher; Venerable Instructor.

Shakti: Universal energy of the active Feminine Principle; the Creative Power of the Manifest.

Sheik, Shaikh: The Master, or Chief Instructor, or Superior Guide of an order of Sufi dervishes.

Shiva: Third member of the Hindu Trinity known as the Lord of Destruction; however, He is also known as the Lord of the Totality of All-Being.

Shunyata: Emptiness, Nothingness; Silence; the ultimate Reality as Void, or Voidness.

Siddhi(s): Psychic powers attained through intense training and ascetic discipline.

Sishya: Pupil, disciple of a Murshid, or Pir (Sufi Master).

Sita: *("Furrow")* In early India, she was known as a fertility, or agricultural (Corn) Goddess, since the repositories of seed known as *furrows* were regarded as the earth's regenerative organs. As the wife of Rama, she is the very essence or light of femininity, the gem of womanhood and the jewel of virtue; she stands to His right, and is strongly devoted to Him; she symbolizes spousal loyalty, fidelity and love; and is the "substantial Shadow", and perfect reflective Light, of Rama.

Spanda: The Primal Pulse, or Pulsation of Creation; the Heartbeat of the Universe; the throbbing Beatific Bliss of Existence.

Subramanya, Skanda, Karttikeya, Murugan: The name of Shiva-Parvati's youngest son; handsome and powerful, he is brother to Ganesha, and holds the position of Supreme Commander of the Army of the Gods; his consorts are Devasena and Valli.

Suksham, Sukshama(s): The various vahanas, or vehicles of expression, surrounding the Soul; for example, the etheric envelope, the astral body, the causal casing, etcetera.

Sushumna: the central main energy channel located along the spinal column; it connects the base chakra to the Brahmarandhra at the top of the head; associated with the upliftment of the fiery essence.

Swaha, Svaha: A ritual bowing and honoring often accompanied by prayer, or invocation, following each offering, during sacrificial ceremonies, such as ritual fire practices.

Tamas: Quality of passivity, inertia, darkness.

Tapasya: Purification through sacrifice, penance, and self-discipline.

Tara: A popular deity in Tibetan Buddhism, said to have issued from the tears of Avalokiteshvara in order to help him in his Task; she embodies the feminine aspect of Compassion.

Tat Tvam Asi: 'That Thou Art God'; that is, God, or the Infinite.

Tyaga: Sacrifice, renunciation; and the eventual, disciplined dropping of all form-related predilections.

Vishnu: Lord of the Universe, Second Lord Creator, and Generator of All; Lord of Sacred Wisdom, Lord of Water, Lord Maintainer, the All-Pervader. The second Divinity in the Hindu Trinity whose role is to preserve and aid in the evolution of mankind.

Wali: A wandering Sufi saint.

White Tara: Born from the tears of Avalokiteshvara, the Buddha of Compassion; she grants long life; her three facial eyes represent the three doors to liberation (the three emptinesses) and the other four on her palms and soles symbolize the four immeasurables (love, compassion, joy and equanimity).

Woden: A later Germanic form of Odin, (Norse); with his constant thirst for Knowledge he became the wisest of Deities; he is also known as the mightiest of the warrior gods; blue-cloaked, he wears a wide-brimmed hat and carries with him a magic spear (his warrior-wizard aspect); he corresponds to Jupiter and to Zeus, his Roman and Greek counterparts.

Wyrd, Urdh: Teutonic Goddess of Destiny; Chief of the Norns whose Divine task lies in directing the winds of Destiny, in regard to both mortals and gods.

Yama: The God/Ruler of Death in the Vedas.

Yamantaka: a Mahayana Buddhist deity; one of the eight Dharmapalas, Protectors of the Teaching of the Buddhas; 'Yama' is the name of the god of death, and 'Antaka' means 'terminator'…'the terminator or defeater of death'.

Yogi: One who practices yoga and undertakes its disciplines out of desire for Yog, (Union).

Yoni: The feminine, receptive principle; the female sexual organ; the original Creative Source; the doorway of Spirit descending into the manifest world.

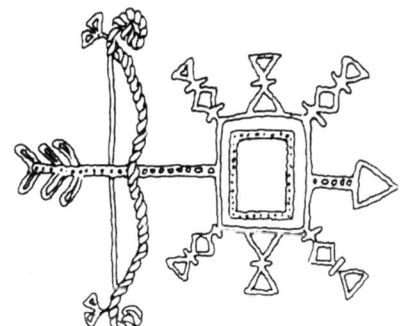

Orange Palm and Magnificent Magus Publications Inc.©
235 René Lévesque Boulevard East, Suite 310
Montréal, Québec, H2X 1N8, Canada
Telephone: (514) 255-8700
Facsimile: (514) 255-0478
E-mail: info@palmpublications.com
Web site: http://www.palmpublications.com